The Grass Swale

Living With Guilt, Depression, and PTSD

Mickey Thomas

outskirtspress
DENVER, COLORADO

Table of Contents

1

Larry

He had taunted and teased me long enough. He was three years older, stronger, and had the mean streak passed down through our old man. The year was 1963; I was in the ninth grade in a school system where Junior High was 7th thru 9th and High School was 10th thru 12th. I was good in sports and becoming popular with the opposite sex. In other words, I was getting used to being respected at school.

I don't remember the circumstances, other than he was trying the same old shit of picking on me. Ordinarily I would give in and try to run away from him. This time was going to be different. I hauled off and hit him as hard as I could and then grabbed hold and hung on. It was a surprise but had no other effect than to make him pissed off even more. He kicked the shit out of me; but from that time forward things were not the same. We began to change from being brothers to being friends. Little did I know—we would only have two more years to enjoy our friendship.

We both played sports and that brought us together once we started playing on the same teams; baseball, football, and basketball. We had moved to Mingo, Iowa in the middle of my freshman year and as we made friends in our respective classes, our friends were brothers, sisters, cousins, etc... If Larry didn't have a date and was just going to town to see what was going on, I started to be invited to go with him.

It was November 29, 1965. Larry and I had just finished basketball practice. It was his senior year and my sophomore year. We were driving home when Larry reminded me we had a 4-H meeting that night. We had moved away during the school year and attended a new high school, but we stayed in the same county. Larry was the President of our 4-H Club, and the meeting would take place about 30 miles away at the Jackson home. Wilbur Jackson was the 4-H Club adult leader, and his family was friends of ours. I don't remember what my excuse was; maybe I was too tired, had homework, or had a test to study for. Whatever the reason was, it will continue to cause heartache for me the rest of my life.

I had a weird dream that night. I heard a woman making that sound where you are not sure if she is laughing or crying. It turned out; she was crying.

My mother got up to answer the door around 2:30 am. A Deputy Sheriff told her that Richard Thomas had been killed in a car accident. At first, she was confused because Richard was her husband and he was in bed. Then she realized that Larry's car was not there.

Larry was killed when a man ran a stop sign at a T-intersection. His car hit Larry's at the driver door and killed both of them. We were told Larry died instantly from head injuries but his car rolled and went end-over-end multiple times before coming to rest upside down in a field. The car exploded in flames and Larry was burned beyond recognition. The sheriff's department traced the car through the license plate number that was registered to dad. Larry and Dad were similar in height and weight, causing the mistake in identity.

Mom woke me early that morning, and it was difficult to understand what she was trying to say but I noticed that Larry's bed had not been slept in… All I remember now is that I never cried. I was in shock because of guilt. I could have prevented his death. I could have changed this terrible tragedy just by going with him that night. I know I was only fifteen, but I understood the timing it took for those cars to meet in that rural area at that split second. You could stand at that intersection and throw rocks all day long as cars went by and you would be lucky to hit one. Only a second would have made the difference between living and dying. I could have; I would have made that difference. In my dreams/nightmares, both sleeping and awake, I have been riding with Larry and we see the car go across the pavement onto the gravel road. Or, we would go past the intersection and I could see the car lights coming in the distance.

My high school was like a large family. With only 99 kids from freshman grade through seniors, everyone knew each other and most were related in one-way or another. When I returned to school I was met with silence as I walked through the halls. A group of my friends would be talking and laughing at a story, but all conversation would stop as I approached. It took many months before others felt comfortable with me. As if it was not normal for me to laugh or have fun. No one meant to exclude me; it is just the way people react.

2

Boot Camp

Bob Gannon and I were good friends in high school and still are. We keep in touch every few months. We decided to join the army on the two-year buddy program. I had gone to Central College, a division III School, to play baseball. While I was there, I decided to walk on the freshman basketball team. God knows I wasn't there to get an education. One of my high school coaches had gone to Central and felt I was good enough to make the teams. I made both squads, so between practice, games, and Bridge games with my dorm hall buddies, I didn't have enough time for classes and studying. Discipline was not a strong suit of mine.

Bob wasn't doing well at Iowa State either, and we both being 18, were old enough to sign the Army papers without parental consent. I quit my summer job about two weeks before we were scheduled to go in. I was just about out of money and a place to live; Dad was kicking me out of the house because I had quit college. Now that I am a parent, I understand how mom and dad felt about my choice. They had already lost their oldest son at 18 years of age, and now their second son, at 18, was going into the service. At the time, it meant a tour in Vietnam and it was not something they wanted to face. Of course, I only thought of myself and knew I would go in the service for two years then come back and finish college. Just about that time, the Army notified Bob, the two-year buddy plan had been dropped, and we would have to go in for three years. Bob went down to the draft board and off he went into the Army as a draftee.

It was two or three days later that I heard he was gone, so I went to the draft board and said, "I am ready to go."

"Son you'll have to wait until next month to volunteer."

"What the Fuck!"

I had no place to stay and no money to get there. So, to the recruiters I went.

As I went down the line, Army, Navy, Air Force, everyone said the same thing; three or four years of enlistment. Then I came to the Marines. The recruiter said they had a two year enlistment that would end soon. He tried to discourage me, because no matter what I scored on testing I would be sent to the infantry. I decided I had no choice, even though the recruiter told me I would regret the decision within two weeks. I wasn't sure what he meant; all I know was it only took the first day in boot camp; MCRD, San Diego, to find out.

I've heard the marines who went to Parris Island Boot Camp refer to MCRD as "The Hollywood Marines." Obviously, they had never met one of our Drill Instructors (DI), a corporal. Later on, we heard a rumor that he had been as high as a Staff Sergeant, but he had been demoted twice for striking boot camp attendees (we were less than worms until we graduated boot camp). If seen by an officer, it can lead to a Court Marshall; so most of the striking takes place behind closed doors, in the DI hut.

The DI was about 5'6" inches tall and reminded me of a black Popeye. His arms seemed bigger than his legs and his chin was jacked up to one side whenever he spoke. The first words he spoke were, "How many of you white boys can't take orders from a Nigger?"

Now mind you, I grew up on the farm land of central Iowa and had never seen, in person, a man of any color other than white until I was about twelve or thirteen. Our 4-H Club had a Soil Conservation Officer, who was African American, come speak to us. I don't think any of us paid attention to what he said; we just looked at him in amazement because of how different he looked. Since then, I had only been to a few county fairs and a goat-fucking contest, but I knew better than to raise my hand on that question. Okay, I had never been to a goat-fucking contest; it is just a figure of speech.

Evidently, two of the boys were not as worldly as I and they raised their hands. The DI didn't seem surprised these two boys raised their hands, he just asked, "Could you two come with me?" He walked over to the nearest Quonset hut and opened the door as both white boys went inside. The DI followed, closed the door, and for the next few minutes all you heard was a lot of banging, crying, yelling, cursing, and more crying; then silence. The door opened, and the DI stepped out as he adjusted his hat.

"I'm going to ask this question one more time. How many of you white boys can't take orders from a Nigger?" No one raised their hand. These boys catch on fast. He never expected to get all the racists, just the stupid ones.

I don't know what happened to those two boys. Some say they would be sent off to something they called CCC. I don't recall but it could have stood for Corps Correctional Camp. I heard they would dig holes in the sand all day and exercise during breaks. At the end of two weeks they would start back at day one of boot camp. I bet they never raised their hands again.

One of my regrets after starting boot camp was being so tall. At 6'3" I was one of the tallest and was put at the front of the line in 4th Squad. That made me squad leader. Little did I know the consequences of the honor. Let's just say, the Drill Instructors and I met way too often. As it turns out, if one of the 20 or so guys in your squad makes a mistake, it becomes the squad leader's mistake. So the squad leader and the guy who screwed up would be invited into the DI Hut for counseling. This consisted of your stomach being used as a punching bag by a DI, while the guy who screwed up looked on. When the DI finished his counseling, the squad leader would start counseling his errant squad member. One thing I learned quickly was if your counseling wasn't good enough to suit the DI he would counsel you again. I would usually catch on after getting the shit kicked out of me.

We found out later the first two weeks did not count for training because they were still getting enough recruits together to complete all three battalions. I was getting the shit beat out of me and it didn't even count. I also found out after boot camp that recruits in the 1st and 2nd training battalions were never touched by their DI. But, 3rd battalion was "Old Corp" and felt a recruit would learn faster if they expected they might be killed at any time, especially the Platoon Leader, Four Squad Leaders and the Rear Platoon Guide. All six of us found out when all hell broke loose the week we went to the rifle range.

Each area of training turned out to be a competition between platoons. Up to that week our platoon had won every ribbon given to the "best" platoon during that particular training event. On the week of the rifle range you "pre-qualify" on Wednesday with the final qualification shoot on Friday. Wednesday night the platoon was called together and told to sit down around the Staff Sergeant. The guides and squad leaders were invited inside the DI area and stuffed into a shower meant for one. One at a time we were pulled out of the shower, put up against the wall, and used as a punching bag for the two Drill Instructors; both were wearing shooting gloves on each hand. I guess they felt the gloves would soften the blows to us, or maybe they were concerned about hurting their hands. I am pretty sure they weren't concerned about hurting us. As the 4th squad leader, I was the next to last out of the shower. As the screaming and pounding took place, I had time to think about what was going to happen.

After each of us was beaten, he was then thrown out of the door for the rest of the platoon to see. The Staff Sergeant was calmly and quietly telling everyone that we had not done what was expected of us; our platoon was in last place at the end of pre-qualification. This beating to their leaders was punishment for their performance and that the platoon needed to shape up before Friday.

Then it was my turn. I don't remember passing out, I just remember the screaming Drill Instructors and getting the wind knocked out of me; then waking up with one of the Drill Instructors slapping me in the face. I must have gone down too fast, and they believed I was faking; they picked me up and put me back against the wall and started beating on me again. I didn't pass out this time, and when they were finished with me I was thrown out the door to join the rest of the group.

I'm not sure if we ended up in last place but I know we didn't win the ribbon that week. Even though it was painful to lie on my stomach during Fridays shoot, I ended up with an "Expert" score. At least the beating had the expected effect on me.

The rest of boot camp was just a blur of many visits to the DI Hut for counseling. But I have to mention some highlights; the bed wetter, the wrist cutter, and the guy who claimed he was gay. I am not sure if any of them were valid or just acting schemes to get out of the Marines. Everybody wanted out of boot camp but three guys came up with some pretty strange ideas on how to do it.

First was the bed wetter. Maybe he thought he would get sent to medical or wherever a bed wetter goes. But the Drill Instructors had an Anti-bedwetting plan. During the night a recruit is assigned to "fire watch," a shift to patrol the huts in case of an emergency. The fire watch was assigned to wake up the bed wetter every hour on the hour and march him to the latrine, stand there for 15 minutes, then march him back to his bunk. This went on for at least 2 or 3 nights and he was cured. He was probably cured the first night but the Drill Instructors wanted to make sure.

The next guy decided things were so bad he was going to end it all by cutting his wrists. He was taken away in the middle of the night bleeding. The next day, there was an attempt by a Marine Officer to make it look like someone gave a shit. Now what are you going to say when asked about your treatment, especially when an officer conduct-ed his interviews within ear shot of others in your hut and the Drill Instructors. What I knew was "Officer Concerned" already knew what the issues were and made a show that someone cared; Bull Shit. We knew he would be leaving and we would be back in the loving care of the Drill Instructors. By the way, we were told the recruit would recov-er from his wounds and would start with another unit at the same stage of training as when he went to the hospital. To prove their concern for our well being, we later received instructions by the Drill Instructors on how to cut your wrists if you seriously wanted to kill yourself.

There is no other way to tell about or introduce this next "get out of boot camp plan" other than to tell how it went down, no pun intended. We were called into the DI hut, as normal, wondering what had happened now and who was getting the beating.

One of the recruits from another squad had announced to the Drill Instructors he was homosexual and wanted to go home. This was a few years before the "don't ask don't tell" philosophy. The Drill Instructors, curious as they were, felt he should prove it. Another recruit, picked by the Drill Instructors, was about to be the person chosen to be the receiver of this proof. The recruit was told to pull out his penis so the act could begin. As I told you before, I was just a farm boy from Iowa and had heard about these things, but to my knowledge I had never met a gay person. I certainly had never thought about what it meant or imagined what I was about to witness. When I tell you this guy seemed excited, anxious, and couldn't wait to get started, I mean it. When the DI said, "Go," this guy was almost foaming at the mouth. The receiver was not as anxious, matter of fact; I think he wanted to vomit. I don't remember how long the Drill Instructors allowed this to go on but they stopped the guy's fun. The DI then turned to all of us witnesses and said, "Pull em out! He is going to start at the front and then work his way down the line." Thank God I was the 4th Squad leader!

"If you let him touch you, you're going to the same place he does."

Needless to say, the demonstrator was still excited and crawled on his knees toward the first Platoon Guide. It took about three or four kicks to his head to lessen his excitement. He never made it to the first man in line. The rest of us just stood there with our dicks hanging out. The Drill Instructors finally put a stop to the demonstration before the guy got killed. Where he went next I don't know, other than to the hospital. We just didn't see him again.

By the time boot camp graduation occurred, I was exhausted from meeting all kinds of new people and having such new experiences. I know my stomach was tired of being used as a drum. But I have to share how the Marine Corp changed my eating habits before I leave the boot camp story.

Now my mother will tell you I was the pickiest eater there ever was. The cooks at school used to ask her how or what I would eat at home. The Marine Corp never cared. That first night of getting our heads shaved, uniforms and boots fitted, and our infamous meeting with the DI, we were marched off to the chow hall. Most of us had not eaten anything since the day before but still were somewhat squeamish about what was being put on our food trays. I didn't recognize anything by vision or smell. The rule was that everyone had to stand at each table with food tray in hand until everyone had gone through the line. When we were told to sit, everyone sat down to check what was on the plate. In less than twenty seconds the Drill Instructors were yelling.

"Get up and get out! Go! Go! Go!"

In other words, we didn't get to eat our first meal. By the time our second visit to the chow hall came we were starved. No one gave a shit what was on the plate; the plan was to get something down as fast as possible. Even at that, the Drill Instructors didn't let us get the meal down completely. Up and out we went again, not sure what we just ate but glad we got something. The next meal would have been funny to watch. I'm sure the Drill Instructors had seen it over and over with each new class. When the Drill Instructors said sit, you would have thought you were at Coney Island watching the hotdog eating contest. Food was flying down everywhere. From that point on we were given enough time to eat a meal but no one ever took a chance, especially if the Drill Instructors were in a pissed off mood and that was most of the time.

I want to revisit one more beating before I get to boot camp graduation. It wasn't the last one but one that clings to my memory. Normally on a weekend things weren't as hectic, especially on Sunday. Only one DI stays with the platoon so things quiet down until Monday morning. But, on one weekend toward the end of boot camp, a DI who had something against me was on duty. For whatever reason, he went out of his way to find one of my guys screwing up so he could counsel me. One Sunday night the DI was sneaking around the 4th Squad hut looking in the windows. He saw someone whispering to another guy in the rear of the hut. The DI came roaring into the hut wanting to know why I couldn't keep my people in line.

"Who wants to take charge of this squad?"

One of my guys stepped forward and declared he would. The DI took relish in watching this guy tear me up. Rumor had it he was a golden gloves boxer from Texas. The DI declared the guy squad leader, and that was it. The next morning when the Staff Sergeant came in and called everybody into formation, I was standing at the end of the squad and the new squad leader was in my spot. Staff came down to the end and yelled.

"What the hell is going on Thomas?"

"Sir, I was replaced by the Sergeant, Sir!"

"Get your ass back to Squad Leader; now!"

"Sir, yes Sir!"

The DI wasn't there because he had worked the weekend, the best I remember. But I am sure he didn't like the conversation with Staff on his decision to keep me the Squad Leader. Of course he came up with other reasons to counsel me before the end of boot camp.

The last week of boot camp was a complete turnaround. The Drill Instructors started inviting us Squad Leaders and Guides into the hut to chat and joke around telling us this had all been for our own good. The main purpose for this was they knew they could run into us some time later during our tour in the Marines and hoped we would only remember, the good times.

Graduation was such a relief. My platoon had won most of the competitions so our platoon flag looked good with all the ribbons we had won. All the platoon guides and squad leaders of each platoon graduated as Private, First Class, something to be proud of. The best recruit in each platoon, based on testing and athletic scores, was made a Private, First Class, and issued a set of the dress blue's uniform.

3

Advanced Infantry Training (AIT)

Off we went to AIT on Camp Pendleton, North of San Diego. Things turned around for everyone because you were now a confirmed Marine and treated completely the opposite of boot camp. AIT was delayed for me and some other unlucky souls. We were pulled out of ranks because we had won the honor of working in the mess hall for the next two weeks. I don't recall anyone else from my squad in boot camp being picked, so all went on to AIT and I was left behind. But you meet new friends and this is where I met Travis, a big white boy from Baton Rouge, LA. I had seen Travis and knew he had been in one of the other platoons in boot camp. The first day Travis got into a fight with one of the Marines in week two of mess duty. Everyone goes through in two weeks, but Marines are changed every week so there are always the guys that have been there a week to show you what needs to be done. Travis was probably pissed from boot camp treatment and didn't take kindly to how he was spoken to by someone his rank. From that point on I knew Travis was a good one to have on your side, so we became friends.

Mess duty was uneventful simply because we did nothing but work and sleep. Up each morning at 2:30 am and in bed each night around 10 pm. As you can imagine, 2:30 came damn quick, and the work was monotonous. Get everything ready for breakfast for the AIT units; after breakfast pull out all tables and chairs, clean everything, then put them all back for the lunch hour. After lunch, take out all the tables and chairs, clean everything, then back in with the tables and chairs for the evening meal; after everyone has eaten, out with all the tables and chairs and cleaning preparation for the next morning. Clean ourselves up then in bed around 10 pm. The second week was better because all the shit jobs went to the new guys coming in and you knew you were on the last few days.

AIT was a blast, literally. We got to shoot mortars, throw hand grenades, and shoot the LAW which was a one man, easy open bazooka. The M60 Machine gun and the M79 Grenade launcher were my favorite. The M79 was nothing but a sawed off shot gun that launched grenade size ammo that you could watch as it went to its target.

I don't remember how, but the AIT instructors chose me to be the leader for this AIT unit. It was an honor to be chosen but only lasted for a few days. A Marine, who was a lance corporal, transferred in and took my position because of his rank. I went into one of the squads and enjoyed the chance to just be one of the guys.

Travis and I went through AIT together and enjoyed hitting the beaches between Oceanside and Long Beach California. Never back to San Diego; bad memories from there.

One Sunday while I was in AIT, some of us caught an interior base bus to the beach area on Camp Pendleton. I was not feeling well and after walking down the beach, I laid down and feel asleep. When I woke up everyone was gone, and I had missed the last bus back to AIT base area. I don't have any idea how many miles it was through the desert but I took off walking. As I walked the paved road, it began to turn cold, and all I was wearing was jeans and a T-shirt. I began coughing and getting sicker as I walked. I felt I would die during the night because I was still miles from the base and no chance of getting a ride. But, as I was about to give up a vehicle came toward me, turned after passing me and stopped. A man driving a cab had made a decision to check out the beach area for riders and picked me up. I told him I did not have money for the fare and he said not to worry. He could see and hear I was sick, so he took me to the base clinic. It turned out I had bronchitis, and it kept me in my cot for at least three days during training. Where did that man come from and who sent him to take care of me? I would have a similar event happen years down the road.

Travis and I were split up at the end of AIT. Scout Sniper trainers went through the unit and spoke to anyone who shot "expert" in boot camp. I thought; sure, what the hell, sounds like fun, I'll train to be a Sniper. The AIT unit went on in preparation for the next move, Vietnam. I headed to Scout Sniper School, which was also on Camp Pendleton.

4

Scout Sniper School

Scout Sniper school was fun. Pretty much all we did was practice shooting the Remington 700 all day. After about three days everybody had black, blue, and yellow bruises from their shooting shoulder to the waist. A few would have cuts or bruises around an eye from getting too close to the scope. The 700 packed a good kick and could bite you if you didn't pay attention. The main thing about shooting any great distance is learning to use "Kentucky Windage;" in other words, an educated guess on how much the distance and wind may affect your shot. You trained in two man teams; a shooter and a spotter. The spotter's job was to see where your shot hit so you could adjust the next shot. The 7.62mm match ammo was designed to be the same size slug and same amount of powder to have little variance between shots. It was all up to the shooter to get it right depending on distance and the amount of cross wind if any.

My greatest shot did not come until years later when my family was visiting my parents who lived in Monet, Mo. at the time. They had a home on the edge of town with six acres of pasture in the back. Their pasture butted up to a neighbor's land that had an old shed for hay or equipment storage. Mom asked me if I could shoot a ground hog that lived under the shed and would come out each day and dig up their pasture, looking for grubs or whatever they eat. I asked about any guns and dad came up with an old single shot 22 rifle with straight sights. I asked for ammo and all he could find was two 22 short shells. It wasn't long before mom started yelling from the kitchen.

"He's out there! Get Him!"

I went out on the back deck. The house sat up on a hill and the elevation fell down toward the pasture and shed. I estimated the shot to be around 130-150 yards and about a 40 foot elevation change. I told my wife, Hope, to watch with binoculars and see if she could tell where the shot hit so I could adjust with the second and last shot. From that distance the ground hog was just a dark spot. I looked behind him and found a line of trees. There was no wind, so I used a tree directly behind the ground hog. Then I went up the tree and found where it branched. This was how I aimed and could not see the ground hog in my view. I shot hoping my wife would see where it hit but mom's reaction said it all.

"You got him, you got him, you got him!"

When I reached the ground hog, he was lying on his back but still twitching. I rolled him over, saw where the shot had creased his head, and simply knocked him out. Probably the greatest shot never recorded. I should contact Ripley's on that one. If the shed is still there we could verify the distance, but all witnesses were family, so I don't know if that would be official.

I want to bring up one event that occurred during Sniper School. It may put me in the crazy category, in some peoples mind, but it happened and everyone there was a witness to the event. We were out on the night shooting range and were using the Starlight Scopes for the first time. It was a clear night, without a moon, with mountains as our backdrop. Starlight Scopes were used by both the person shooting and the spotter to help adjust the next shot. You are able to see objects in the distance with a green haze as the only color. All of a sudden there was a bright ball of light hovering along the foot of the mountain range. The weird thing was; with the naked eye nothing could be seen except the black outline of the mountains and there was no sound. I would guess we watched this object of light hover through the mountain range for over five minutes. It would disappear around a mountain or foothill then reappear again. I was watching it when it stopped moving then slowly started gaining altitude, then it became a flash of green light as it went up and away as if it was a shooting star; but away from earth instead of toward it. Our Gunny went berserk.

"No one saw anything! I am not doing the fucking paperwork involved in this. Do you understand?" That was the end of the night range. We packed up and back to our quarters we went. Call it what you want, but it was unidentified, flying, and an object. The fact is, there was no sound at all and the idea we would never have known it was there without the Starlight scopes.

After Scout Sniper school I was able to spend a few days with friends in Long Beach, CA. Diana Beard, Larry's girlfriend at the time of his death, had married. Her husband, Lowell, was in the Navy at the time. We enjoyed a trip to Sea World while I was there during Christmas of 1969. Again my luck was bad because I was pulled out of the ranks for two weeks of guard duty. This pulled me away from the unit again and any other friends I made while in Sniper School. After guard duty, I was assigned to a waiting list of Marines to be sent to Vietnam. The Marines stopped sending whole units at a time and simply sent a number of needed troops who were then assigned to units around Vietnam as needed.

I remained on Camp Pendleton until August of 1970 when I received orders for Vietnam. I was not allowed to go off base my last weekend because I was caught with a fake ID. An acquaintance had used his skills to create fake ID's for him and me to get into night clubs along the beach areas we visited. I only remember using it once to get into the Golden Bear in Huntington Beach. As it turned out the group playing that night was the Nitty Gritty Dirt Band. That was prior to their hit *Mr. Bojangles,* but they were a tremendous show. Even worth losing my last weekend off base before leaving for Vietnam. Somehow one of the Sergeants had heard about the ID's and requested to check my wallet. He could have had me thrown in the brig for a while and court marshaled me, so I know he gave me a big break.

5

Shots and Sex

By the next week we were flying on a major airline to Fairbanks, AK. It was dark, so I did not get to see any of the Alaskan scenery. After a short layover, we were on to Okinawa for jungle gear, shots, and sex; in that order. I believe we were there for three days and given $25 for night entertainment.

Today, I have a beautiful wife of 40 years at the time of this writing, with four beautiful daughters. I need to cover this part of my journey but let me tell facts without any embellishment, thank you.

First, the shots; which never bothered me but one of them went into the hip and I know it had to affect my performance later. It felt like a square needle going in, and turned that side of your ass black and blue for a week or more. It was humorous to watch people going through the line where at one point you were getting a shot in each arm at the same time. Some guys passed out before they even got there. Just watching was more than they could handle.

Now, on we went, to the nightlife and our last chance for sex before going off to war. I don't remember the city we went to or the street where most of the bars were located or even the names of any of the bars. But each bar had plenty of pretty girls to sit with you, drink your drinks, and rub on those shot areas to make them feel better. Ok; other areas too. At one of the bars we decided it was time to get laid. There it is; that's what I wanted because I had never been laid before. Heavy make-out and heavy petting was the most I had ever done; and only with a few girls at that. We were all thinking the same thing; get laid in case we die. I knew I had to at least have that experience with a woman in case I never made it home. Or, make it home but without the ability. At least I had a plan. I was going to see how I liked the first girl and if so, I would go back to her the next night. If I got anything afterward, I wanted to at least know where I got it.

My plan was delayed as we were getting ready to leave the bar. I had bought the last round of drinks and the waitress disappeared without giving me change back. I was pissed because my plan of getting laid was out now that the money was gone. There were 4 or 5 of us together and we walked up an ally from the bar to a place called, Central Hotel. I volunteered to hold any personal items and cash outside the hotel seeing how I was broke. We had no idea of what dangers awaited inside and this way at least none of them would lose their wallet or cash. As I waited outside the hotel, an older woman came out of the bar we had been in and up the ally. She stopped and asked, "Why you no go inside?"

I explained my money loss from the bar down the alley and she said, "No problem, you go in for free."

"Sure!" I said. "How much is free?"

Again, she said, "No problem, I own bar and hotel, I let you have free!"

"Ok, but I'll wait out here till one of my buddies come out." When one came out I turned over the belongings and went inside. Ma Ma Son was true to her word. When I came back out of the room to the lobby, Ma Ma Son was still there.

"You likie?"

I nodded my head, "I likie."

"You come back tomorrow night and get again for free." She was my kind of business woman.

This lady had the best strategy in marketing you could ask for. Turned a negative into a positive and she knew I'd be back with more friends. What a lady! So, back the next night, same girl, free again. What a wonderful world.

6

First Night in Vietnam / Introduction to Bravo Squad

Now, we are on to Vietnam via a major airline, landing in Da Nang on August 27, 1970. At some point everyone was brought together in a group and assigned to our units. I had checked to see if there were any openings in the Scout Sniper Unit. There were none, so I was assigned a regular infantry unit. I was going to 2nd Battalion 5th Marine Regiment, Echo Company, 3rd Platoon, Bravo squad.

On August 30th some of us were loaded onto the back of a truck and our stop was a place called An Hoa Combat Base, in Quang Nam Province, southwest of Da Nang. We arrived in enough time to be fed a hot meal and were assigned a tent and a bunk. I had not been issued a weapon yet at this point. That night I was awakened when a rocket attack was launched by the Viet Cong on An Hoa. There was small arms and machine gun response from our compound but I had no idea where to go for cover. I just stayed in my cot and was back to sleep as soon as the commotion ended. The next morning during breakfast, the word was an orphanage was hit. Years later I would find a unit chronology on the internet with confirmation of 15 killed and 45 wounded. That would be my first situation where the civilian population was the victim of war; but certainly not the last. That was my last meal for quite some time, served on a plate, while sitting at a table, in the shade of a mess tent.

Later that morning I was issued my M16 rifle and ammo. I was put on a truck with a few other Marines and down Liberty Road we went, headed east. One of the guys in the truck had been "in country" for awhile. He was shirtless and had sores all over him. He had not shaved for quite some time and you could tell he was miserable. I found out later he was my 2nd LT, 3rd Platoon Commander. Three of us were dropped off at the 3rd Platoon Compound along Liberty road: The LT, a new Marine assigned to the weapons squad, and myself.

3rd Platoon of Echo Company had lost two Marines who drowned when the unit crossed a river around the 4th of July. I was their replacement along with the other Marine who went into the weapons squad. 2nd Platoon was set up farther East along Liberty Road, with 1st Platoon further down.

Bravo Squad consisted of "Ham" who was Squad Leader, "Strick" was Point Man, "Irish" was the Radio Operator, and the rest of the squad consisted of "Oscar," "Tennessee," "Cher," and others I can't recall. I can see their faces but can't remember their nickname. From that point on I was known as "Tom." My squad had been out on a night patrol/ambush the night before so they were not assigned for anything that day or evening. We spent most of the day inside a bunkered hole lined with benches for sitting or lying down. Cards were played, and I was introduced to everyone and overheard some of what was going on in our area. Our mission was to protect Liberty Road going between An Hoa and Hill 55, and conduct day and night patrols within our assigned area. 1st and 2nd Platoons were set up in similar compounds farther down Liberty Road with maybe a mile or more between us. Our compound also had a 109 artillery gun which was used to shell known enemy areas in the mountains nearby.

After spending the day down inside the bunker, we went up to stretch and prepare our evening meal. After we had eaten, and it got dark, I was tired from the travel and lack of sleep the night before. No one had gone into the bunker to sleep. I learned later, they were waiting on me to go first. Down I went to lay on one of the benches and covered up with my Marine issued camouflage blanket. It wasn't long before I heard something scurrying around in the bunker, then more and more. The noises got louder and all of a sudden something ran across my legs and then across my head. As I came running up the steps, out of the bunker, everyone acted as if nothing was going on. I am sure there was a bet on how long I would last in the bunker. No one said a word, but the rookie had learned his first lesson. The bunker belonged to us during the day and the rats at night. We slept on the ground around the bunker.

Diarrhea hit within the next two days. I don't know if you ever read the book, *50 Yards to the Outhouse,* by Willie Makit and Betty Don't. I didn't make the ditch latrine built on the outer edge of the compound. My one issue of jungle pants was filled with liquid shit. I had to take them off to wipe myself clean. I was told the first day, water was at a premium because we were in the dry season and was for drinking only. I had nothing to wash the pants, so I used dirt to soak up the shit then let them dry in the sun. Next I scrapped off the dirt as best I could and I wore them that way until I received clean clothes; about a week later. No one wanted to get too close and I don't believe I was included in any cards down in the bunker until the clean clothes arrived.

The next two weeks or more was the same hot, dry days, and the slightly cooler humid nights. I was taught on my first night ambush that everything you learned at AIT regarding setting up an ambush was thrown away. No L shaped ambushes; just a straight line and close enough to reach out and touch the next man on either side. This formation allowed one person at each end to stay awake as the others slept with a change of watch every hour.

7

Marine Killed by Artillery Shell

One morning in September, 1970, we had just come into the compound from a night ambush and were taking off our gear. A huge explosion went up about a 1/4 mile down the road. In the smoke and dust that went up at least fifty feet, there appeared to be an object that looked like a body. Then we saw Viet Cong; about four or five of them, run out from the tree line nearby. We opened fire with our M16s as the Viet Cong ran back into the trees, but we were too far away for any accuracy. Bravo Squad ran down the road as fast as we could to see what happened. As I approached the blast site I noticed red spots; like rain drops all around the area as if from a quick and short rain storm. There was no breeze and the still air had a strange smell: the smell of death. I am told a body is made up of mostly water. The drops splattered on the grass, the dirt, and leaves of the surrounding plants were the combination of fluids and blood that had once been inside the body of the Marine.

The area was what we called a day post where two Marines would spend the day on guard. They were responsible to observe any enemy movement, radio the information, and hopefully be able to get back to their compound. This day post was manned by the 2nd Platoon. During the night, the VC had carried in a 109 artillery shell that had not exploded on impact in the mountain range. The VC had hard wired a blasting device to the artillery shell, ran the wire back to the tree line, and waited for the day post Marines to show up.

One Marine had been out in front of the other far enough that he saw the shell as he arrived. As he went to look the VC set off the shell. He must have been standing right over it when it exploded, lifting him into the air and tearing him to pieces.

Ham had already reached the Marine and I could tell it was bad from the look on his face. As I walked past I looked at his body but my brain would not allow me to register what I saw. As I looked back to where I was walking I was shocked awake when I almost stepped on his left arm, which had been severed at the elbow. I walked on to set up a perimeter for the helicopter landing and sat next to Cher.

"Did you see that?" He asked me.

"I don't know."

"You had to, he was right there in the open."

He went on to say the man's head was gone just above the eyes, his body was cut in half at his waist and his lower torso and legs bent backward on each side of his head. Every ounce of fluid in his body had been mixed and scattered like rain.

As I sat there waiting for the chopper, I was glad Ham did not select me to help gather what body parts could be found. The air was still thick with the smell as I fought off the urge to vomit. All I could think about was that I knew the man had just died but his family and friends did not know. I knew the shock they would go through and the time required to heal emotionally. The visions and thoughts of that day will remain with me as long as I live.

The hamlet of Phu Nhuan was not far away, and it was known a band of VC was using it for supplies. Probably the same group who had set the artillery shell. A small recon group composed of a few members of Bravo squad observed a band of about seven VC move into the hamlet just before dark on the night of September 15th. Problems with their radio caused the recon team to travel back to the 3rd Platoon compound during the night. The plan was to move Echo Company around the hamlet during the early morning hours in hopes of trapping the

VC. The villagers were probably still asleep when all hell broke loose around them at dawn as Echo Company opened fire. Another platoon, probably 2nd platoon, went thru the village huts one by one looking for the VC. I don't remember hearing that any were present during the attack nor if any of the villagers were killed but we no longer had any problems with the VC while we were in the area.

The next few nights while we were out on ambushes we saw "Puff the Magic Dragon" doing its thing in areas around the hamlet and nearby mountains. Puff was the nickname for a plane set up as a gun ship with lots of fire power. The ones at Da Nang in 1970 were AC-119 Stingers. Puff could be heard as a normal plane would sound but then its guns would open fire and the tracers would look as if red hot lava was pouring from the sky. Word was, the rounds could cover every square inch of a football field. If you were in its path, there was a zero survival rate.

8

Humor

I want to get away for a while from the dark matter and try to insert some humor, even though someone might not agree that humor existed. But that is what we do as humans; we try to laugh away our fears, anxiety, and all negative feelings. That is what stand-up comedians do for us. They take things in our lives and look for the humor in them. People in the military or police, fire department, or EMT's can understand what I mean by finding humor to release stress. My wife finds humor easily, and I wonder if it's because she has been married to me for 40 years.

Bravo squad was on a day patrol for some reason (I don't remember) but I remember the day in great detail because of how dirty and dry we were. We had not had a shower or washed for probably a month. But we came upon a large pond of water that some local village kids were swimming in. I don't know if the water was a natural pond or man-made via bomb, etc. What I remember is we split up so some could stand guard while the others bathed. We even had some soap someone had been carrying.

I was butt naked and had dove into the water and was standing waist deep in the water, soaping down, when the next thing I know something swam between my legs; pushed between my ball sack and the tender part of the leg; the area that almost never sees sunshine and grabbed a hold of me. I am sure I probably screamed like a baby and broke some sort of record getting out of the water. To my horror, a leech had taken hold of this tender skin and would not let go.

I know you can imagine how shocked and sorry everyone was for me. It probably took five minutes before anyone could stop laughing and try to help. One guy wanted to use a lighter whose flame was being blown around in the wind. My whole focus was to hold my manhood away from the leech in case he decided to move to a new and sweeter location. And of course I was protecting myself from the idiot with the lighter. Finally someone lit a cigarette and touched the leech which fell to the ground. I was bleeding from the suction but no one volunteered to put a bandage on the area. Some comments were made that I should have kept the leech because it was bigger.

A lot of stress was released on that little episode. But we learned how to bathe in a Vietnamese pond. Dive in and get out fast. Soap down then dive in again, swim like hell and get out. No leech problems for the rest of Bravo Squad that day.

The next humorous event involved me and the fact I almost drowned in about three feet of water. We were on a night patrol and the M60 Machine Gun man was with us. That meant I was carrying M60 ammo cans, one over each shoulder. The straps stayed on the shoulder of the flak jacket if you crossed each strap to the opposite shoulder. They stayed in place and the weight was evenly distributed. This night was the darkest night you could imagine. There was no visible horizon and you could hardly see your hand held out, much less the man in front. Sometime during the patrol we moved onto a dike that was not very wide and between two rice fields. At one point as I stepped with my right leg I hit a washed out area, and I lost my balance going into the water on my right side. The problem was my left leg caught on the dike and I could not get my right leg under me to get up. I was pulled under water by the weight of the ammo and could not get them off because they were crossed. I'm making all kinds of noise spattering and splashing. By pushing with my right arm in the muddy rice paddy I could just break water to try to get a breath! My savior was the guy behind me; he did not see my left leg and tripped over it. He was able to reach out and grab my left arm to drag me back to my feet. With all the noise any VC within a mile would know we were there. The guys around me got a quick laugh out of it. Little did they know that my wet condition would prepare me for Ham's choice for the ambush set up. We lay in the rice paddy with water up to our waist with our shoulders and head leaning on the dike. Everyone broke out their lightweight blanket to put over their heads in an attempt to keep the mosquitoes from getting to our faces. You could hear the swarm of mosquitoes and you could feel the leeches pushing against the pants and shirt looking for a way into the warm body for dinner. Some were successful.

9

Monsoon

It became time to move from our compound on Liberty road, probably the end of September. 2/5 Marines headquarters began the transition from the An Hoa Combat Base and moved into Firebase Baldy. This move was completed by October 15, 1970. From this point on I would be sleeping in a shelter created by taking your poncho and snapping it together with a partner's poncho. This would be our shelter from the hot sun or pouring rain. Once the monsoon season began, the problem with too much sun or heat disappeared. I recall one day when we were still at the Liberty Road compound. Tennessee and I were sent out to a day post similar to the one where the VC had set the artillery shell. The day post is essentially a suicide post because the enemy knows your purpose is to report their movements with your radio. If there is a plan to attack the compound their first objective is to silence the day post. Anyway, Tennessee and I were on the day post and it had been hot and dry forever. But, along came a thunder storm and a torrential down-pour. Tennessee and I were like two little boys out in the rain acting as if we're talking a shower. Then it started to get cooler and cooler and we were soaking wet. Tennessee and I huddled together in our make shift tent and froze our asses off. Screw the lightning or the VC; we thought we would freeze to death.

10

Finding Reggie

I'd like to take time to get into our daily routines and living conditions because I believe it took as big a toll on me as did the stress of wondering when the next attack would come. When will someone hit a booby trap? We moved out of the An Hoa Basin and into the foot hills and mountains of Que Son. Each night we would set up a make shift compound with fighting holes dug and our poncho tents next to them. 2/5 had begun Operation Imperial Lake in an attempt to disrupt NVA supply routes and safe harbors. We may stay for a day or two in each location but the goal was to reach a location where we could dig in and stay for a week or two. From this area we could run our day and night patrols looking for Charlie (VC). At some point during our digging fighting holes, someone found a human skull. It did not appear to be a grave, just a place somebody's head landed after a 1000 lb bomb hit nearby. Anyway, we named the skull Reggie; we placed it on a pole, and carried it with us as we moved from location to location. Reggie became our Bravo Squad banner. God forgive us our sins.

Then the rains came. At the time, I knew it was raining hard, but did not realize we were hit by Typhoon Kate on Oct. 15, 1970. I've already told you about being wet and cold but that was just for a day. Now we would be wet, cold, tired, hungry, pissed off, and anything else you might want to throw in yourself. We had set up in the mountains and we must have stayed in this location for at least two weeks. The trails between our tents became flowing streams of mud. We would dig trenches around our tents in an attempt to keep water from running through it. Even though you were wet, you could keep warm by lying back to back with your partner and feed off each other's body temperature. Yes, I said back to back. This was a mountain, but it wasn't *Broke Back Mountain*. We spent some days just trying to get a fire going to dry our clothes and boots. Then a down pour would start and put out the fire. Most of us had problems with wet feet; the more serious ones would be sent by helicopter to Fire Base Baldy to dry out for a day or two.

At some point probably about two months after I had joined Bravo Squad, Irish replaced Strick as point man and I took over as Bravo Squad radio operator. It was toward the end of the hot/dry period and we had been picked up by helicopters and flown to Fire Base Baldy for a two day "rehab." What it meant was two days and nights of rest, a shower (with hot water if you were one of the early ones), hot food served on a tray, cold milk, and sleep on a cot inside a real tent. This time allowed us to recoup and get drunk at least one night. Beer was made available, maybe two cans of Budweiser then it would be gone and Black Label would have to do. We didn't care; it was a relief just to have the time off. From this point on with 2/5 Echo Company we would spend about 25 to 28 days in the mountains then back to the fire base for one or two days recoup. Echo Company rehabbed at Firebase Baldy on November 15 and December 6, 1970 then January 3 and January 30, 1971.

After our stay on the Fire Base we packed enough rations for a few days, and we would walk out of the base to get to our first nights temporary site. I remember this day specifically because I was loaded down with supplies and had the radio, an additional 25 lbs plus, the radio man carried red and green smoke flares to add to the weight. We walked the entire first day and into the evening before reaching our destination. During break periods I would find a tree to back up against and lower myself to a sitting position. It would take a hand from two buddies to get back to my feet. Once we reached our destination, we would set up a temporary base camp and work day and night patrols. After a few days or weeks we would break camp and head to a new area; sometimes by chopper, sometimes by walking.

During one patrol, in an area referred to as "Arizona," Irish had turned a corner and not more than 30 yards across a small ravine, walked a VC crossing a large rocky area. Irish and the next guy in the squad opened fire on the man, who according to Irish, he fell to the rock and his body jumped and jerked from the rounds being fired. When they stopped firing the man lay motionless. Irish called back to Ham that we had a kill and Ham requested me to radio the kill to the platoon leader. As soon as Irish had looked away, the man jumped to his feet and disappeared into the bushes nearby. Irish and others opened fire again, but we never found a trace of the VC. I don't know about you but I believe the man instinctively knew to go down and flop around as if he was being hit. How he wasn't hit is beyond me. I'm sure he had some liquid shit to clean up later that day.

In addition to making life wet and miserable, the Monsoon period played hell on getting re-supplied in a timely manner. The rains created emergency re-supply operations for elements of Hotel and Echo Companies. On one of the days, we were in the mountains, fighting the rain, hoping the choppers could get in. We were to get hot Turkey dinners with dressing, mashed potatoes and gravy; Thanksgiving, 1970. It didn't look like they would be able to land but somehow they did. It was raining while we went through the line to get our meal. Rain in the mashed potatoes, but it did not dampen our appreciation for the meal.

One particularly tough time we were dropping to half rations to stretch out supplies. The mountains can get locked in for days at a time leaving us vulnerable to food and ammo shortages, but also to the inability to call for an airstrike if needed. After dropping to half rations we would have to cut back on patrols because of the lack of energy to hike the mountain terrain. The point man paid a price because many times he would have to cut a path through jungle vegetation and would have to be relieved or a break taken. The radio was a problem not only for its weight but it would get caught on vines which took extra energy to pull away or get help from someone to get untangled.

One time we were in a particular rough mountain area with little or no pathways. We were to be picked up and moved by helicopter to a new location but we could not find an adequate spot for the chopper to land. The Marines used the CH46 helicopter that had two sets of rotors, one at each end, so it took more open space to land. At one point we found a large bomb crater on a side hill. We dug out this area for half a day just trying to allow the chopper space to sit the tail end down. When the chopper came in, the pilot hovered and then lowered the tail down to the crater but one of the blades clipped the outer edge of the crater. The chopper was damaged, and it took off down a valley and out of sight. I don't know whether the chopper made it back or at least to an open area but we were still on the mountain, running short of supplies. We ended up getting supplies dropped to us then we walked off the mountain following stream and river pathways.

I want to take some time here to talk about the beauty of Vietnam. I have walked through a great deal of the Northern part of what used to be South Vietnam. Since then I have seen much of the US, Caribbean, and Hawaii, and would go to Vietnam any time to vacation. The scenery of the mountains stays with me as well as the chill of the cold mountains streams we would bath in and drink from. The people are wonderful. They deserve the peace from war over the past forty plus years. Entire generations have grown up not having to hear the sounds of war. Hopefully this will continue for generations to come. Vietnam has the resources and is on its way to become a major tourist destination.

During Operation Imperial Lake, Bravo Squad came upon an area of caves that had been vacated by the VC/NVA. These caves provided the protection against bombing raids and many were concealed from view both from the air and ground. While searching the area we broke up into teams of two. Oscar and I had sat down next to a cave opening during a break. Oscar saw a small piece of black plastic protruding from the ground and started to pull it and carefully dig around it with his hands. It became obvious that it was a large piece of plastic that was used to protect something. By the time we were done digging we had exposed what turned out to be a 30 caliber anti-aircraft gun, probably Russian made. As other members of Bravo Squad appeared, Oscar, and I had already started to put the gun pieces together. When completed, we had assembled a gun that was in remarkable condition and probably ready to fire. Somewhere, some of the guys have pictures of that gun with members of Bravo Squad. I remember seeing the gun again during one of our Fire Base visits. It had been mounted on the back of a jeep. I believe the gun was to be sent back to Oscar's hometown, somewhere around Minneapolis, and donated to a local Veterans Group in Oscar's name.

11

Kenny

One day, I was approached by our Platoon leader and told to get my gear packed; I was going back to the rear on the supply chopper. When I asked why, I was told not to ask questions he couldn't answer. Within the hour I was off on a flight without knowing why or where I was going. The chopper did not land at Firebase Baldy; it went straight to Headquarters on Freedom Hill near Da Nang.

When I got off the chopper my questions were answered; there stood my cousin, Kenny Meyers, with his huge smile. Kenny was a mechanic in the Army and was based somewhere south of Da Nang. We knew we were in Vietnam at the same time, but had no idea where. Kenny had talked his way into a five day or so pass and hitched hiked his way to Freedom Hill. Once there, he had to find Echo Company and then convince them to bring me in for a couple of days. What a surprise! Even though I was not allowed to leave the base, I was free from any duties that required me to remain sober. The details are blurred but I know we had a great time visiting and I was able to get hot food and a shower. Kenny and I had our pictures taken by a photographer on base and had them sent home. Kenny had one blown up of us together. The first and only time I saw that photo was at Kenny's funeral service. Kenny died of a massive heart attack at the age of 45 during a family reunion on July 4th. Thanks again Kenny, for the honor of knowing you. Two days with Kenny then back to Bravo Squad.

12

Killer Team

Over the next few weeks two events are clear in my mind. The first was a "Killer Team" put together to accompany two Scout Snipers over a 3-4 day period. Our job was to provide backup for the Snipers while they set up in an area looking for enemy movement. I was the radio operator for the team. We traveled most of the night; going through mountain terrain you would probably not walk if you could see how far you would fall before stopping.

The team returned to the Platoon about three days later with no contact with anything, much less the enemy. I just remember it rained most of the time and I was kept busy trying to keep me and the radio dry. The other event was the day we dug holes in preparation for an air strike. Word was there was NVA moving on the other side of the ridge. We dug in simply because the airstrike was going to be 500 to 1000 lb bombs dropped by Phantom Jets. The fun part was watching each jet as it approached the valley. The newer the pilot the more daring and lower he flew. That was our take on it. The pilot who was short, (close to going home) stayed high and let the bomb go so early it was a wonder it didn't hit us. We started calling out a rating for each plane with the winner coming in low, dropping the bomb then climbing straight up with a roll or two. After the air strike we crossed the ridge and moved down into the valley looking for the results. No enemy found, but a 1000 lb bomb will shred a forest better than a wood chipper. As we traveled through the mountains, damage from other bombing raids was everywhere. Some areas hit with Napalm were still coated with a waxy film. Other areas were completely barren of living plants or trees where Agent Orange was used. Of course, we didn't know anything about Agent Orange at the time, especially its long range health issues it would cause for many soldiers as they grew older. Bad news was heard over the radio on January 10, 1971. A Gulf Company unit hit a booby trap injuring two marines. The Executive Officer (XO) chopper was in the area for observation. The XO ordered the chopper to land to medevac the wounded marines. When the chopper landed, the XO and the Echo Co. Captain walked toward the wounded marines. According to the report, neither was wearing protective flack jackets, and the XO struck another booby trap, killing him and our Captain. I had seen our Captain just one time, but I was impressed by his presence and leadership and proud to know he was our Company commander. It was hard news to take and even harder to maintain morale in the field.

13

Transfer; A Very Sad Day

There came another day in early February, 1971, when the Lt. stopped and told me to get my gear together; I was leaving on the "Supply Chopper." Only this time it wasn't because of a visitor! I was told that 2/5 was going home in a few weeks and anyone with less than six months (in country) would have to stay. I found out later I missed the cut-off date by about two weeks. I and the weapons platoon marine, who arrived the same day as I did, would be transferred to 2nd Battalion, 1st Marine Division and assigned to a new company. This was a sad moment because I would be leaving Bravo Squad but not going home was the hardest to swallow. I said my goodbyes and left on the supply chopper. We landed near Marble Mountain, headquarters for 2/1. My plan was to request a transfer to a Scout Sniper unit; but that plan soon changed. While standing in line at a chow hall, I spotted a familiar face; Travis was sitting at a near-by table eating with a group of Marines. We shook hands as he followed me along the line, catching up on why I was there. Travis immediately wanted me to join his unit, and I agreed. He contacted his company commander and the next thing I know; I am a member of Hotel Company. I did not know then that Travis and the rest of 2/1 with more than six months in Vietnam would soon be heading home as well. We just had a few weeks before Hotel Company and 2/1 would be turned upside down.

To this day I don't know what platoon or squad I was in with Hotel Company; Travis would have to answer that question or maybe a little research could solve the question; the point is, it doesn't matter. The rumor mill is active no matter where you are; R&R (rest and relaxation) would be stopped and those with eligibility would not be allowed to go. You became eligible at six months and I met that date just shortly after joining Hotel Company. I went ahead and put in for R&R even though my choices were limited and did not include Taiwan, the place I really wanted to go. A squad member had just returned and his stories of the beautiful women there had me dreaming of my visit; wet dreams I'm sure. My poncho tent partner probably had second thoughts of getting paired up with me. As it was, I was scheduled to go to Hawaii; not a bad place for beauty, but most of the soldiers went there to meet their wife. No wife would mean I would have to rely on my sophistication to find a woman and get laid; which meant I wouldn't get laid. That, or spend more money for one roll in the sack than all five of us spent in Korea. Asian destinations provided a bonus with each night stay, a woman. Most hotels had a bar that included 30-40 women wearing a number. You simply went to the bar after checking in and picked the woman who grabbed your interest. She was yours 24 hours a day for the rest of your stay. If for some reason, you didn't get along, you simply returned her to the bar and made another selection. You could have had a different one for each night if that was your pleasure.

Just a few days before leaving on R&R, Hotel Company, had been assigned special duty as a quick response unit in case another unit needed help. After a friendly village was attacked by the VC, we were flown to the site to set up protection against further VC attacks. When we arrived, we set up a temporary compound just outside the village. Word came to us from the villagers that another attack was coming; "VC come tonight at midnight." As it got dark we finished digging our fighting holes, setting up our poncho tents, and eating a cold meal. No fires tonight. As we sat talking quietly and waiting for something to happen, a rocket, launched by the VC, hit so far away from us we didn't realize they were shooting at us. But then the VC opened up with automatic rifle fire; it was the "ack ack ack" of AK-47s. Three of us dove into a fighting hole made for two and came up firing at the VC. I was stunned as the M16 muzzle next to me exploded in my left ear. No one in our compound was hit during the attack that night and I left the next morning by chopper for Marble Mountain in preparation to leave on R&R. I found out later the VC attacked again that night, killing one of the ARVN (Army of the Republic of Vietnam) assigned to our platoon.

When I reached Marble Mountain, I was informed my sea bag was destroyed during a flood of the storage facility. All my belongings, including name and addresses of personnel from Bravo Squad, Echo Company, 2/5, were gone. My civilian clothes, wallet, and driver's license, were destroyed. My plan had been to rent a vehicle in Hawaii and live in the car while stopped at public camping areas. You know, to save money for the more important things. But, without a DL I was not able to talk my way into a rental car. I arrived on a Wednesday and would be leaving back to Vietnam the following Wednesday. I was told I couldn't even take a driver's test until the following Monday to get a temporary license. With my plan destroyed and my left ear still throbbing from the muzzle blast two days before, I grabbed a cab and told him to take me to a nice place to stay. Of course, he took me to one of the most expensive hotels on Waikiki Beach at that time, the Ala Moana Hotel. The hotel included a large shopping center where I bought one set of civilian clothes (a colorful shirt and bell bottom slacks). The rest of my money would have to cover the room (no woman included), food and a few beers. Once I checked into the hotel and reached my room, I saw a real bed for the first time in over a year. It rained almost every day I was in Hawaii but it did not matter; I only ventured out of the room a few times. Other than going into the mall to buy my clothes and one walk on Waikiki Beach during a break in the rain, I never left the hotel. All my meals were by room service and I went to a bar in the hotel maybe three times for a beer. The rest of the time I slept, ordered food via room service, watched TV, and then back to sleep. It did not matter whether it was night or day. The bed was a wonderful place after sleeping on the ground for six months. The time went quickly, and then it was back to Vietnam where home was under a poncho tent.

By the time I returned to Hotel Company, my platoon had moved on from the village. It was not long after this that Joe and all the other marines with more time "in country," would head for home. This created another re-organization of Hotel Company. A few others like me went from one of the least experienced marines, to one of the most experienced. The next three months in Vietnam would prove to be the hardest and scariest time for those of us left behind.

14

Bucky

I made a decision to not get too close to anyone in my unit. But, when you share a poncho tent with someone, you can't help talking about family and friends back home. My new partner was a marine nick-named, Bucky, because of the obvious smile full of front teeth. I never kept notes of his real name or hometown because of reasons previously mentioned. What I do remember was his family operated some kind of tree service business either in New Hampshire or another state in the Northeast. I remember his stories of climbing trees to trim or doctor them.

Because of my experience with the radio, I was assigned to be the platoon radioman, reporting directly to the Platoon Commander, a Lieutenant. Bucky gained interest as he listened to me operate the ra-dio ordering supplies or filing daily reports. At some point, he asked if I would train him on how to take over the radio position. Once ap-proved by the platoon commander, Bucky took my position. Neither one of us realized I would get the position back within a short period.

We had been in VC territory for a short period when they blew up a bridge during a daytime convoy of trucks carrying ARVNs. Small bands of VC could travel at night along tree-lined rivers. These areas gave the VC the protection to move at night and hide from our day and night patrols. They used this method for attacks such as the bridge, or rocket, and small arms attacks on villages that became too friendly with the US military. Other villages helped the VC with supplies and information regarding our location and movements. One such informant was a young boy who could not have been much older than twelve. The story was, his brother was a VC, and the boy had lost one of his arms when a booby trap exploded as he was trying to learn to set it. The boy, along with two others about his age were caught trying to set a booby trap on the trail used by Marines in the area for making mail or supply runs to a local highway. I had moved to the point man position, and I saw them while leading a day patrol for mail one day. They were playing cards along the trail as we passed; probably using the cards to cover up an explosive device. After we passed, the boys tried to set up a booby trap on the trail for our return trip, in hopes one of us would step on the device. Lucky for us they were caught setting the trap by an ARVN patrol they did not see coming. The twelve year old was being interrogated by the ARVN leader upon our return. They knew his brother was a VC, and they wanted the boy to give up his location. The ARVN had wired the boys fingers with a military field phone. When the phone was cranked, it sent voltage through the boy making him cry in pain. At some point, the boy evidently agreed to lead a patrol to the VC location.

On March 18, 1971, a squad was chosen for the patrol and the LT. decided to go along. This meant Bucky went with them as their radio operator. The patrol was doomed from the beginning because the boy decided to lead them through an area heavily booby-trapped. I am positive the boy knew where each device was located and could avoid them. I was told later, Bucky hit one of the devices as he attempted to cross a small creek. Because of the weight of the radio it made it more difficult for him to jump over the area. While those in front of him jumped over the creek, Bucky stepped down next to the creek and hit the booby trap.

The explosion was heard from our location but news of what happened would not come until later when the rest of the squad returned. I spoke to the corpsman who gave medical aid to Bucky before the medevac arrived; the wounds were critical. The corpsman was concerned of Bucky losing one or both of his legs, his groin area was seriously damaged, and one side of his face was mangled. To this day I do not know if Bucky lived, and if so, how serious his wounds were. Maybe someday I'll find out that he is living a good life. Our Lt., walking behind Bucky, was hit in his chest and stomach areas and seriously injured. Also, our Staff Sergeant, an asshole, was hit in one of his thumbs. He would be eligible for the same Purple Heart that Bucky and the Lieutenant would receive. Such Bullshit!

15

Operation Scott Orchard

I became the radio operator again. Our next mission, according to our leaders, never took place, and we were not to discuss it with anyone in our letters back home. We didn't know where we were until after the choppers dropped us into the jungle. We were in Laos looking for a prisoner of war camp. Records that are now declassified show it was called Operation Scott Orchard. I believe we were there for three days but did not find any of our guys. We found areas that had been abandoned within a day or two, but no prisoners. While we moved through the jungle I was in the second squad from the front so when we took a break I slid down a tree and fell asleep almost immediately. I was awakened by gunfire at the front of the patrol. It seems the point man and a couple of other Marines were sitting next to the trail when two enemy soldiers came around the corner of the trail. The first was shot and wounded before he could escape but the second man got away. Because we were in the jungle, the enemy soldier was medevaced by lowering a stretcher by cable from the chopper, just above tree top level. Any other enemy soldiers were well aware of our position by that time.

The rest of the day was spent walking the jungle trails to select a place to set up camp. The next morning when I rolled out of the poncho tent, my partner asked "what's that on your face?" As I touched my face, a leech dropped to the ground. He was full of blood, so my touch was enough to make him let go. When you stop and think about all the snakes crawling around at night, the leech was a better alternative.

16

Cluster Fuck

At some point, by the end of March, our squads were reorganized as more Marines went home. For the next two weeks or more, another experienced Marine and I shared in either the squad leader or point man position. We were told some new Marines from Okinawa would be joining our unit in the near future. These Marines had been playing war games while in Okinawa and were now itching to get into real action. Little did I know what that would mean for our platoon. One of the new Marines, a corporal, was put in charge of our squad. It didn't matter that he had not spent but a day or two in Vietnam; he was put in charge because of his rank. You would have thought the Staff Sergeant would have let him get a few days of patrols before putting him in charge, but he didn't. I told you earlier, the Staff was an asshole.

His first patrol, as squad leader, was a night ambush. Just a quick lesson so you understand something about a night ambush. The squad leaves the compound before dark and not necessarily in the direction of where the ambush will be set up, in case the VC is watching. Everything in the military is by the metric system so instead of yards we walked in distances of 1000 meters, which we referred to as "one click." Therefore, you may go out one direction two clicks, then left two clicks, and back left one half click, then set up the ambush just off the trail. By the time you reach the ambush site it is totally dark.

Everyone lies down in a straight line so you can reach out and touch the man next to you. This allows one Marine at a time, or one at each end, to stay awake while the others sleep.

It is important to be where you are supposed to be because the weapons squad may choose target areas around the compound for mortar attacks. The only place they don't target is where the night ambush is supposed to be. Also, Puff the Magic Dragon may be lurking in an area you don't want to be. So, in the words of Ron White, the comedian, "I had to tell you that story in order to tell you this one."

My squad is assigned the night ambush with our new squad leader in charge. It is the squad leader's responsibility to tell the point man when to change direction and if they need to go left or right. After about three clicks and two direction changes, in the wrong directions, the point man stopped. I was second in formation with the squad leader behind me. The point man and I spoke with the corporal in a calm but firm tone. "Corporal, we are not in the right location for the ambush!" It was already dark and we had at least two clicks to get where we were supposed to be before the weapons folks started mortar attacks. The corporal agreed and we headed to the ambush site in the opposite direction the corporal had told the point man to go. Once at the site, in total darkness, the corporal started setting up some elaborate ambush formation he learned in Okinawa or read about in some comic book. He started to move people all over the damn place. If an ambush would have taken place, no one would know who the enemy was and who wasn't. Again, we explained this fact to the corporal and set up the ambush in a straight line along the trail.

The following morning, upon our return to the compound, the corporal went straight to the Staff Sergeant and complained that the two of us were insubordinate and took over the patrol. When staff spoke to us about it we explained the situation. Whether it went any higher than that I don't know and didn't care. But both the other Marine and I had been mentioned for promotion to corporal, but that never happened. No problem with me.

Because we were so low on experienced Marines, one of the other squad leaders approached me and asked if I would join his squad for a night ambush. Most of his squad was new transfers, and he wanted someone else along for the ride. And what a ride it would turn out to be. The ambush was to be set up not far from a village that also contained an ARVN compound. The plan was to set up along a trail that followed the tree line near a river. Also, parallel to the tree line ran a cemetery. A Vietnamese cemetery consists of mounds of dirt because the people are buried in a sitting position. We set up the ambush about 20 yards outside the cemetery and parallel to the trail. During the night, there was an attack on the village by the Viet Cong, with rockets and small arms fire.

As it got closer to daylight, I woke up and could see the end Marine who was on watch. We both saw the VC at the same time. We quietly woke up everyone and got ready as a single VC approached. I could see his silhouette and that he was carrying something on his shoulder; which turned out to be a rocket launcher. He must have been involved with the village attack and was now on his way to safety before light. As he came closer he blended into the tree line in front of us. We were all guessing where he was when we opened fire.

When we stopped shooting the squad leader had the radio operator call our compound for flares to give us some light. Then he asked for me to go with him to approach the VC. The first flare was off target enough to cause long shadows from the tree line. I approached from the left while the squad leader moved in from the right. Just as I saw the VC lying face down, the flare flickered and went out. As we yelled to the radio operator for another flare the VC opened fire with an automatic pistol. In a few seconds the VC had planned to take someone with him as he prepared to die. The next few minutes could only be described as a complete "CLUSTER FUCK." The squad leader and I both dove face first to the ground as the Marines behind us opened fire on the VC. It still amazes me today how neither the squad leader nor me were hit by either the VC or the Marines behind us.

As the next flare lit up the sky I fired on the VC again as he went over one of the burial mounds. He was dragging one of his legs, probably being hit during the initial ambush. He had fallen into a low area which protected him from the ambush. Somehow, the VC made it to the tree line as we swept the area until daylight. There was no sign of the VC or a blood trail anywhere. We gathered up his rocket launcher and headed for the compound; the entire ambush a failure. Whether the VC lived or crawled into some bushes to die, I'll never know; but I have 1000 versions in my nightmares.

The Staff Sergeant was not happy when we returned; we had a chance for a kill and it failed. He noticed a funeral procession about two days later from the local village, to the cemetery. He thought he had a way to confirm the kill. Staff put two and two together and decided it had to be a funeral for the VC. Luckily, I was not chosen to be one of the guys doing the digging. Under cover of night, while the rest of us set up watch positions, the new mound was dug up to find the body of an old man. Asshole!

One day while on patrol we heard an explosion in the distance but did not see what the source was. While taking a break we noticed two villagers coming toward us carrying something between them. As they neared our location it was obvious they were coming to us for help. Two women carried a third woman who had struck a booby trap, and both legs were nearly blown off. She had lost a lot of blood but was still alive. Our corpsman gave aid as best he could while the call was made for a medevac. One of the women looked like someone in her late teens with beautiful dark eyes peering out above a veil that covered her face. I had not seen this habit before and I was wondering why she wore it. From her reactions I felt this girl must be the daughter or related to the woman who was seriously injured. When the medevac arrived the force of the wind from the rotors answered my question about the veiled girl. The wind blew the veil up exposing the fact she had no face. She did not have a nose, lips, or teeth, just a hole. All three women were taken on the chopper. I've always hoped that doctors tried to help her with plastic surgery.

17

The Grass Swale

Probably a month had gone by since the reorganization of Hotel Company. I had turned over the radio operator duties to one of the transfers and the corporal put me as the permanent point man. Some time later, one of the transferred Marines spoke with the corporal about becoming the new point man. I was more than willing to let him have it. The corporal agreed, so I worked with the Marine until he had conducted both daytime and nighttime patrols, and he was assigned point man for the squad.

Not long after he took over as point man, we received information that a group of five or six VC were crossing the river not far from our compound. Our squad was chosen to try to intercept the VC. I was approached by the corporal to walk point for this mission. I don't know if the Marine begged out or if the corporal did not feel he was prepared, but I did not hear any complaints from him about the change. With this being a daylight mission it would be imperative that I see the VC before they saw me.

As I walked along the path near the river, I started to see signs that booby traps were ahead. The VC would use any three items to warn other villagers of booby traps. This could be three rocks, three sticks, or any three items piled along the trail. The items did not mark the location of booby traps, they simply warned villagers not to go any farther.

As I approached the trail's entrance into the tree line it was obvious where the booby traps were. The dirt path stopped at a grass swale area about 20 feet in length as it went through heavy shrubs and turned to dirt again on the other side. It was obvious the grass swale would contain booby-traps, and I had to make a quick decision on how to get through, to overtake the VC. I chose to go along the very right-hand side of the swale, staying away from the center. I explained to the next Marine and corporal to have each man step where I did. I took smaller steps than normal so everyone could see where to walk and started to breathe again once I made it through the swale. The path turned to the right, and I continued to move slowly, watching for the VC, giving time for others to get across. I had not gone far when the silence was shattered by an explosion behind me. As I turned, a large column of dirt and smoke rose into the air. "What the F…"

The VC could not have been far away, and the surprise was over. The fifth man in line was lying in the middle of the grass swale with part of one of his boots gone and shrapnel tears in his pants up through his groin. Guess who? The Marine who had taken over as point man evidently thought he saw something and stepped closer to take a look. Boom!! Bad decision.

The corporal and radio operator crossed back over the swale as a medevac was ordered. Not only did we have to get the Marine out of the path area but he also was caring the demolition bag full of explosives. Somehow another Marine and I were able to get the demolition bag and the wounded Marine back across the swale without hitting another booby-trap. Because our position had been exposed, we abandoned the mission and return to the compound when the medevac was completed. Marine chronicles have identified this date as April 19, 1971.

On April 25, 1971, came word from the Staff Sergeant that our platoon would be used as a block as another platoon from Hotel Company pushed the VC out of the tree line from the other end. As we set up positions, the Staff Sergeant, and I ended up together, not far from the booby-trapped entrance to the tree line. We were not 50 yards away, and it was in sight of our position. I warned the Staff Sergeant we would have to stop our Marines leading the push before they reach the grass swale. I explained it was where we had tried to go through and that it was booby trapped. The Staff Sergeant ignored my warning and said, "They will get through, they have Kit Carson Scouts leading the patrol." Within a few minutes the patrol, led by two KC Scouts, came around the corner toward the grass swale. As they approached the booby-trapped area, one scout went down the far left side and the other went along the right side. The first Marine walked right down the middle hitting a booby trap on his first or second step in. The Staff Sergeant never said a word, and we sat silent while the medevac was called. So much for the fucking Kit Carson Scouts. As the helicopter landed it blocked our view of the area. Within seconds another explosion with dirt and smoke rose behind the chopper. Seconds later another explosion, and this time the Staff Sergeant groaned. After what seemed an hour, the chopper took off. Years later, a review of unit chronologies, showed that five Marines were injured that day: one emergency, two priorities, and two minimal evacuations. Another thousand dreams of—why?

I had been insubordinate with the corporal when it was necessary why didn't I do the same with the Staff Sergeant? It was so unnecessary and could have been totally prevented. Who planned the sweep and how could they not be aware of the booby trap hit just days before. I don't remember any conversation with the Staff Sergeant, but I know my hatred for him remains to this day. And I cannot stop blaming myself for what happened. I should have run to the location and stopped the patrol. I should have helped get the wounded Marine through the swale, preventing the other explosions. I will remain haunted by that day and my lack of action for the rest of my life. *Father, please forgive me for what I have done and what I have failed to do.* I doubt if the wounded Marines would forgive me once knowing it could have been stopped.

18

Freedom Hill

The following weeks were the same routine day after day, but we became aware we were moving closer and closer to Da Nang and Freedom Hill. One of the last nights ambush patrol was so close to Freedom Hill that we could see the lights of the base. I was thinking how close we were to going home. As I looked at the lights they began to blink on and off. I focused on the area and saw the outline of people walking along in front of us. Because we were so close to Da Nang, we had been told to radio information about any movement and get permission to fire. By the time permission was granted the people were long gone yet we opened fire anyway. As we fired, my weapon jammed, and I was unable to feel anything blocking the chamber. Unable to fire my weapon, I simply turned over on my back and waited for the firing to stop. As flares filled the sky, there was no sign of the enemy. They were lucky that night and so was I. It would not have been good to have been in combat without a weapon. The next morning I was able to see that the head of a shell casing had come off leaving the casing in the chamber. Later that day we walked out onto a highway and sat to wait for trucks that would carry us on to Freedom Hill.

19

Okinawa and Home

From that point, it was a matter of days until we were flying United Airlines back to Okinawa on our way back to Camp Pendleton and the world. Those last days in Vietnam are a blur because I could not believe it was actually happening. We were getting ready to leave; we were going home. All those months and days before, I had felt as if home was too far away. You could never dwell on home because it would drive you crazy. We did receive letters, tapes, or even a food package whenever we were in one place long enough to receive them. There was also a lonely feeling when mail call came and you didn't receive anything. I was one of the lucky ones who had friends and family who sent letters and packages but it still created a hollow feeling if your name was not called. Some guys never received anything, ever.

Going home meant another trip through Okinawa and another night on the town. I was ready to head for the Central Hotel, but one of the Marines had another place he said was great. He and I went inside while the other buddy waited for the Central Hotel. He made the right decision. I was given a room with a girl who was very young and obviously scared to death. Nothing happened, and I said nothing to the owner not wanting to get the girl in trouble. Also, I didn't want my buddies to know what did not happen.

When we arrived at the Central Hotel my Marine buddy was

paired with the same girl I had 10 months earlier. I knew she would take good care of him, and later, his face proved me right. Just a side note before moving on: Prostitutes, in Asian countries at that time, may have been the sole breadwinner for the family. Prostitution, if ran as a legitimate business, with health checkups given to both clients and employees, would solve more problems than any of us could imagine. Just a thought.

The rest of our stay on Okinawa was to give up our jungle gear and have a few classes about how to adjust back into the world. Little did we know how we would be treated once we arrived. We flew home making a stop in Honolulu but were not allowed to leave the terminal. After a layover of one to two hours we were on our way to the US mainland. Once back in Camp Pendleton I received more good news; anyone who had less than four months left on their time in service was going to be discharged and sent home. This time I made that cut off by two weeks and was soon headed home to Iowa.

While in Vietnam, I knew I was fighting on the side of technology and strength, but we would all find out a few years from then that belief and determination in what one fights for would win in the end. Let me say right now and get my political views out of the way; hind sight has shown we did not lose the Vietnam War, our military was gone. We left the South Vietnam people, to fight for their country. We gave them the technology and training but we could not give them the mental strength and resolve needed to win their war. We had spoiled them, gave them a false sense of superiority, and left them. As with any war, old rich men weigh what they have to loose or gain without much concern as to what it will cost others.

20

Welcome Home

As I look back on going home, it was quite different than what you see today. No one you met in airports said, "Welcome home!" The only ones to meet you at the airport were family or friends. I didn't know any different, just get me home and into blue jeans, sneakers, and a T-shirt.

What I missed most besides friends and family was the ability to jump into my car and drive anywhere I wanted to go. No need to worry about where the enemy was; just drive. For almost two years I had taken either a bus or taxi while stateside or walked or flew in a helicopter in Vietnam. What a great feeling of freedom to get into a car and cover vast distances in no time at all.

The summer before I went into the service, I was making good enough money to buy a used car. My dad worked with a man who was trying to sell his wife's car; a 1963 Chevy Impala Super Sport, cherry red, with black interior and diamond studded bucket seats. The car was an automatic on the floor with a 409 cubic inch engine. With a small carburetor, the car ran well but was not set up for racing. It was a great car and dad kicked in what extra money I needed to buy it.

When I joined the service, the car went to my younger brother. I was anxious to take the car for a ride and work out whether it would go back to me or stay with him. It did not take long to make that decision.

When I arrived home, I found the car now had a blue front end, a 283 cubic inch engine, and a three speed manual transmission. My brother had been leaving town one night after school and did not see the truck in front of him was stopped to make a left turn. My younger brother and I never had time to become friends like I had with Larry. He was far enough behind me in school that we were not in high school at the same time. I was off to college, then into the service as he went through his high school years. Upon my return from Vietnam, I had fun being with my brother, trying to catch up on good times. Another friend and I took my brother out to a local party one time and got him a little over his alcohol limit; good times. Also, I remember my father and me going to one of his football games that fall. My brother had a great game and made two tackles in a row during a goal line stand. I believe he also made an interception on a pass into the flat to stop another drive.

While I was in Vietnam, most of my massive paycheck went home for mom to put in the bank. I only kept enough each month to pay for my R&R and to buy a few cartons of cigarettes. The fact we spent most of our time in the bush, allowed me to have about $1400 in the bank when I got home. Off to find another car and I ended up with a 1971, Ford Pinto. Hey, no one knew it could turn into a firebomb in a rear end collision. It ended up being a great car for me and could write a book of its own about our experiences together over the next seven years.

Back to getting home; no parades, no welcome home by strangers. I can only tell it from my perspective, knowing each veteran had different experiences; mostly negative. My world, central Iowa, changed a great deal from September of 1969 to May of 1971. When I left, most guys had short hair and the only drug of choice was alcohol. Many of my friends were now sporting long hair and in a few cases, smoking marijuana. While at a party one night, I was talking to some friends, and a guy came up who knew me but wasn't in the friend category.

He said; "Hey, Mick, where have you been? I haven't seen you around."

"I've been in the Marines and just got back from Vietnam," I said.

The guy asked; "Did you kill anybody?"

"Not that I am aware of."

"Oh", he said.

Then he walked away with an indignant look on his face. I guess if you didn't kill anyone, he considered you a failure at war. He would not be the only one to feel this way. Most people either had a passionate dislike for vets, or didn't give a shit at all. Hey, you know what the white stuff is in chicken shit? Go to the end of the next paragraph to find out.

21

Post Traumatic Stress Disorder

As time went on, the only ones who knew I had even been to Vietnam was someone I felt was a friend. Those friends have remained loyal and were very helpful in my ability to get back to a "normal" life. No one was made aware of Post Traumatic Stress Disorder (PTSD). No one was made aware of Agent Orange and its effect on the human body. There were people aware of both; but it took many years for that information to work its way to the public so we could understand its effects on our lives. (It is just more chicken shit.)

I have been told by a VA counselor that PTSD can't be cured. It is a matter of being aware of it, talking about it, with the knowledge that the memories will never go away. But those memories can be dimmed and less traumatic through understanding and professional guidance. Too many veterans feel they must protect their family and friends by not discussing those experiences. What they need to understand is they must open up and share those experiences to take away its power. The writing of this book has been part of my recovery.

Even though the events took place over forty years ago they can be as clear as an event that is taking place now. Each event I have described has been replayed in my mind thousands of times whether I was awake or asleep. In most replays I have attempted to make sense of what happened or inserted details that did not occur as a way to improve the outcome; but, the outcome remains the same.

I have been told by a professional that you must be present during an event for it to cause PTSD. Call it what you want but events such as the death of my brother and its effect on me will also never go away. In Arnold Palmer's book, *A Golfer's Life*, he describes an event while at Wake Forest, where his roommate and golf team member was killed in a car accident. He had been invited to go along by his roommate, but declined. He describes that event as a "shadow" in his life. I, for one, understand exactly what he meant. My shadow has been darker, much darker. The fact I was not present when Bucky hit the booby trap does not take the anxiety away; what effect has it had on his life, how could things have been different, what could I have done? It could have been me. Why wasn't it? Did it happen to me in another place or time?

22

Change of Attitude

One thing time has changed; my attitude toward the enemy; the Viet Cong. The change has gone from hatred to one of acceptance. That has taken a long time and I totally understand anyone who can't make that step. I was hurt mentally but came back with no physical damage. I would have lived a different life if I had been wounded by the VC or even hit by my own squad members during the night ambush. How would my life be different if I had hit a booby trap going through the grassy swale the first time, or as we attempted to get our wounded squad member to safety. Mitch Albom wrote a book called, *Five People You Meet in Heaven*. After reading his book it made me face my own feelings about the VC who shot at us and got away. I was twenty years old at the time and I'm sure he was probably around the same age or younger. What would I have done growing up in Vietnam? My parents and grandparents would have been farmers just trying to keep their families fed with enough left over to sell and make ends meet. How would I have been affected by the French rule and the war fought between them and those wanting Vietnamese rule? How many of my family would have been killed or wounded fighting such a war? We know what we would do today if a country conquered the US and tried to keep control. I, along with most of you, would be involved in an attempt to take back our country; we would fight to the death.

Imagine the hardships we would have to endure if we were out-manned, out gunned, and had no aerial support of any kind; no supplies available such as clothes, food, and ammunition. Some would fight, some would accept rule, and some would join the enemy forces. What would you do? My thoughts have changed from wanting the VC to have died from his wounds to praying he survived, that he married, and raised a family in peace. I left with the last combat unit of Marines in May of 1971. Could he have survived through to the end of the war in 1975? When the NVA took control would he have been a hero and given a position of importance? I guess I'll have to wait until I meet him in Heaven and we will see how wrong it was for both of us to have been in that situation.

23

Life's Next Chapter

The summer of 1971, I was able to get a good paying job with a local feed company in Grinnell, Iowa. The shift stunk: 5PM to 3AM, Monday through Friday. But, more than that, I worked hard stacking 50 pound feed sacks onto pallets. I got the job because the GM was an ex-marine and I told him I would work there and make it my career. I lied; I already knew I would return to college that fall to NE Missouri State University in Kirksville, Missouri. Each day of stacking feed reinforced my decision to go back to school; using the GI Bill to pay for my education.

One day after getting up and making some breakfast, I noticed two Marines walking to the door. "What the hell do they want?" As it turned out, they were there to give me a Navy Achievement Medal with Combat V. One read the text of the award while the other pinned the medal on my T-shirt. Mom had gone into town for groceries so it was just me and the two Marines. Not much else to say about that. I didn't leave the medal on my T-shirt when reporting for work.

That summer I made enough to buy a motorcycle, a 450 Honda; something I had always wanted. It wasn't a hog, but it was what I could afford and it satisfied my needs at the time. That bike gave many hours of satisfaction; girls like dogs, fast cars, and motorcycles; and put up with those who have them.

I did have a small 80 CC Bridgestone my senior year in high school, but I had to buy it "under cover" through one of my friends, Harold "Oscar" Perry, who was 18 and old enough to make the purchase. I don't think I paid over $100 for it. Dad had refused to allow me to buy a motorcycle, so I kept it in town at Oscar's. I would ride it anytime I got to Mingo and after awhile someone told Dad. After an ass chewing, we took the bike home and before long dad would ride it out to check the cattle or crops. Before you knew it I was riding again. See how things work out sometimes. You just need to remain patient.

I had moved into an apartment with Corky Phillips and Jack Lacey as soon as freshmen were allowed to move out of the dorms. I didn't pay attention to the weather forecast and woke up the next morning after an early spring snow storm. The only thing I could see were the rear-view mirrors sticking out of a snow drift. My Honda lived in our kitchen until all threats of weather went away.

I had met Jack "Lace" Lacey while living in the dorm. Lace lived across the hall from me and my two roommates. He was giving one of them shit about something. I introduced myself and settled whatever the issue was. Lace and I became friends for life and he is God Father to my youngest daughter, Jacqueline. Matter of fact, it was through Lace and his girlfriend, that I would meet some nice women friends with the best and last being a girl named Hope.

24

College the 2ⁿᵈ Time

I saved enough money during the summers to pay for college tuition and books and used the GI Bill to pay for my monthly expenses. The GI Bill provided me $175 a month, and I was able to make it cover my car payment, and living expenses. I still was not sure of what my major would be in college. I felt I wanted to do something along the lines of conservation work and decided to check out Zoology. My plans changed as soon as I met with my counselor and found I would have to take advanced math courses and statistics. Math was not my thing so my counselor suggested a major in Criminal Justice and support classes in subjects such as Biology, Forestry, and Botany.

That was the direction I went and did well in all my major classes. I usually got an A or B in the classes I enjoyed and would just squeak by with a C in the rest. I had an uphill struggle after transferring a 1.67 from my credits at Central College. The military had increased my discipline enough that I was able to do what needed to be done. But not by sacrificing all the joys of life.

Lace and I teamed up with two other friends, Craig Jackson and Dan McCabe, for the rest of our college days. I had known Craig since junior high school in Kellogg, Iowa. My brother, Larry, had died on the way home from the 4-H meeting at the Jackson's home. Craig was three years younger than me, but my previous adventures had put us into the same class. His older brother Danny was also at NEMO attending school. Dan McCabe was from Mt. Pleasant, Iowa, and still lives there today. All of us are a little crazy so we got along great. All four of us were in Criminal Justice so we helped each other with classes. We went to classes most of the time but when the weekend came; it was party time.

One of my favorite stories came early on in 1972. Lace had come to school with his new pet; an Iguana he kept in an aquarium. It seemed fine for a while then it got some sort of lizard disease and died. We wondered what to do with the aquarium and then had an inspiration. We had a hole in the kitchen floor big enough that we would notice a rat stick his head out now and again. We baited a trap using a laundry basket. The bait was set and a string run from the basket to the table allowed us to be ready when the time came. I'll give the capture credit to Jackson; the rat came to the bait and Craig sprung the trap. Now what to do? How do you get the rat out from under the can without getting a bite on the hand? I'll give Lace credit for having some heavy duty gloves and grabbing the rat before he could escape. Who knows how many nights the rat and some of his kin had been prowling around the apartment while we slept? Maybe they even came into our rooms at night to search for food. Anyway, the rat was made at home in the aquarium with a wire screen on top and a rock to hold the screen in place. I can't remember how long we had the rat or if we even named him or her. I do remember its misfortunate end.

As I said before, we were known for our parties so people would just show up any Friday, Saturday, Sunday, Monday, Tuesday, Wednesday, or Thursday to see what was going on. One night we had quite a party going and Lace decided to entertain us all with his skill and bravery. He took the screen off the aquarium and was trying to catch the rat by the tail without getting bitten. I was betting on the rat myself. The ones not amused with this little game were the ladies at the party. The three loudest protests came from three girls sitting on the sofa next to the end table where the rat's home was located. I can't remember who all three were but one was Craig's future wife to be, Gail. A pretty blond who had no trouble telling Lace he was an @#@&XX%. This was already known by most but it didn't affect Lace in the least.

Lace finally was able to grab the rat's tail and lift it out of the aquarium in triumph. What Lace failed to realize is the rat has muscles in its tail and back to allow it to pull itself up and try to bite his fingers. This scared Lace and he let go of the rat's tail, thinking the rat would fall back into its home. But, the rat was able to grab the side of the glass, pull himself up and jumped into the lap of the first girl on the sofa, then the next girl, then the last girl, and over the arm of the sofa and to the floor. There are no words to describe the amount of love lost for Lace on that one event in his life. The noise decibel from all the ladies in the room was the highest ever recorded in such a situation. As word spread that a rat was loose in the apartment, girls started to abandon the party; not even a "thanks for the drinks."

By now, Lace had chased the rat into our bedroom closet, and after slipping on his hunting boots, went in feet first. Between his love for hunting and the alcohol he had consumed, he went in with gusto. He came walking through the remainder of the guests with a rat which looked like it had been quartered and drawn. The three ladies, still recovering from the first shock, went into a sequel of screams and words not normally in their vocabulary. The guests parted like the "Red Sea" as Lace went through the kitchen and out the front door. Good thing we hadn't had time to get attached to the pet rat yet. I still chuckle inside anytime a rat story comes up.

Dan McCabe had pledged Greek his freshman year and was a member of Phi Lambda Chi, one of the smallest fraternities in the country at that time. I believe there were eight chapters around the Southwest and the chapter in Kirksville was the only chapter in Missouri. Jackson, Lace, and I were always invited to parties at the frat house which was only a few blocks away from our apartment. I think we spent more time partying at the frat house until the rat event wore off some and we could get women to return or at least the ones that we dated or others who had no knowledge of the event.

On occasion, I would make a weekend trip back to Mingo, Iowa, where I graduated high school, to see friends. I owe a tribute of thanks to Bill and Paula Maher and Harold "Oscar" Perry, for the many nights of allowing me to sleep on their couch. My parents had moved away from Mingo after I graduated and had purchased 80 acres of land south of Searsboro, Ia. You could not find Searsboro on most Iowa maps at the time. This would come into play in about two years; but I'll tell that story in its proper place. Anyway, I took Lace to Mingo a few times, and he enjoyed my friends as much as they enjoyed him. We had such a good time one weekend that we got separated with no idea where the other was. I guess you have to understand, this was before cell phones; no texting, no way to contact the other person. I know that's hard for some to believe. All I remember is waking up somewhere in Ames, Iowa and Lace was nowhere around. But, I was learning to become an investigator and found a ride back to Mingo, tracked him down, and returned him safely to Kirksville, unharmed, at least physically.

My third year at NEMO, September, 1973, began with a move into another apartment in a large home on Franklin Avenue. Craig, Lace, Dan, and I moved into a three-bedroom apartment on the street level with a large front porch. This would remain our home until graduation two years later.

Lace and I had separate bedrooms with Dan & Craig sharing a third, larger bedroom. We had a nice size living room and a large kitchen to accommodate the many parties over a two year period. Not but two blocks away was a great little diner called "The Blue Moon," that had a great reputation for their cheeseburgers. We helped keep them in business over the next two years. It was one of those places that looked bad from the outside but served great food.

Up to this point my GI bill was covering my expenses, but I was given an opportunity to work three nights a week at a local liquor store, known as "The Alamo." The white stucco building stood alone along Hwy 63 and fit the name perfectly. I worked 5 hours per night from 5PM to close at 10PM for $1 per hour. The owner allowed his workers to have soda's, candy, chips etc. while working. The unwritten rule, as best I remember, was you could take home a six pack or so as long as you kept things reasonable. The take home amount probably was exceeded on occasion but the owner was happier covering the shrinkage than paying more per hour.

The best part for me was the study time I was able to get between customers. I was taking major courses by this time and I put in the time to get either an A or B in these subjects. At some point during the year, Lace turned 21, and he was able to get on the nights I wasn't working. With both of our "take home" benefits, we usually had cold beer in the fridge.

25

Frat Life; Good Time

I mentioned before that Lace, Craig, and I had partied with the Phi Lamb's for two years and we were finally rushed hard that fall to join. Lace and I decided to pledge, but I had second thoughts about dealing with the pledge process and what was called "Hell Week;" the final week. After dealing with Marine boot camp, I felt I would not react well to the mental and physical bullshit from the Phi Lamb actives. But, we had some great guys to pledge with us and the bonding that goes on made it an enjoyable experience over all. I imagine some of the actives who knew me well held back out of respect for my background.

My pledge class worked on creating a natural amphitheater at the rear of the Phi Lamb property on the edge of town. I believe we had 4 or 5 acres to the rear of the house. A wood barn had been erected to have parties and allow people to get out of the weather in case of rain. One end was open such as a cattle shed while the other end was closed off for secure storage and served as a bar area for parties. The barn had electricity, and flood lights had been erected along the pathway from the house to the barn. This location allowed us to play music and party without much annoyance to our neighbors.

We constructed the amphitheater by clearing the brush and thickets down a natural slope that fell away from the barn area. Large trees were left in place for shade and used to set up more flood lights. At the bottom of the hill we built a wooden stage with electric outlets for bands, etc. The seating was dug into the hillside with multiple rows of railroad ties donated by the railroad from multiple areas around NE Missouri. As far as I know none of them were removed from actual working train tracks. When completed, we had a tremendous party area, and it was put to use right away. Future Phi Lambs would appreciate the work put in by our pledge class.

One of the funding projects the Phi Lambs hosted each year was the "pig roast." This was a combined effort along with the "Aggies," the agricultural fraternity on campus. The Aggies provided the roasted pigs while we provided other food dishes, the beer, and party site. For a reasonable price anyone could eat and drink till their hearts or stomach's were content, whichever occurred first? This event was a great money maker and everyone around campus looked forward to a great time.

I believe it was my junior year when my college career came close to ending early. "Streaking" became a popular event around the world for bored people who either wanted to show off what they had or were too stupid to care about showing what they didn't have. Word reached the house one night that "streakers" were under way on campus. Three of us with motorcycles took off with the idea of chasing them down or possibly assist if any females were involved and needed assistance. They might need a means of escape from authorities. By the time we hit the campus sidewalks the streaking had ended, and they were nowhere to be found. What we did find was campus police who were not amused with our use of the sidewalks. We headed for one of the exits by Missouri Hall dorm; the problem was I was last in line to get through the metal pipe opening that kept larger vehicles from driving onto the sidewalks. As the first rider went through a police cruiser pulled up to block the path. Out jumped a man to stop the second motorcycle but was nearly run over as the escape was made. I could have run over the man, spun a 180 and continued the escape, or stop; I stopped. The man turned out to be the Dean of Students and I was provided with an invitation to meet him in his office the next morning.

During the meeting I was given an ultimatum to provide the names of the other riders or be expelled. I declined his offer and was given 24 hours to come to my senses. When the guys found out my situation they went in to meet with the dean and saved me; I believe we were put on double trouble probation until graduation. It was a good thing the dean wasn't aware I had already been down one of the sidewalks the year before with my trusty Ford Pinto. I had decided to make a detour one night between a power pole and its support cable onto one of the women's dorm sidewalks and out onto one of the other streets. I am almost certain alcohol was involved and one of my passengers challenged my driving ability. The following day, a measurement of the pole and support cable confirmed I had a two inch margin of error. Anyway, after the dean's warning, I decided to become an exemplary student and one that any parent would want to date their daughter.

Another major event my junior year was the Phi Lambda Chi National meeting; held that year on our campus. With only eight chapters at that time, and most of them in the Southwest, we all met yearly to compete in sports and party. I have no doubt that all who attended still smile at the thoughts it brings back. We had the perfect site to handle the crowd and the "Aggies" helped again by roasting the pigs and preparing the sides. We provided invitations to every sorority on campus and I estimate we had close to 200 Phi Lambs from the other chapters.

We had a special treat for the party entertainment. One of the Phi Lambs had a great summer job working as a light man for porn movies. This gave him access to some of the professional actresses and one took his offer to come to Kirksville to entertain the troops. With our stage and amphitheatre it was a perfect setting. To come up with the funds to pay for such entertainment the young lady agreed to a sleep over with a lucky winner holding the raffle number selected. She was such a good sport. We even covered the lodging expenses for her and the lucky guy.

The sad part of this story for me was that I was so busy working the event I missed out on her performance. I was on a constant "run here and there" to get this and that, usually more beer, and didn't have a chance to party until it was mostly over. I did hear that one of the Phi

Lambs from out of town had the winning lottery number. Because he was married, he auctioned off the ticket to the highest bidder. I wasn't present for that either. The rich just get richer.

I know everyone had a good time because our final tally was forty-eight 16 gallon kegs and another twenty 8 gallon pony kegs for the weekend.

26

Summer Internship

The summer of 1974, I was lucky enough to obtain a summer job with the Iowa Conservation Commission. The job was located at the Red Rock Reservoir for the Waters Section Officer and entailed enforcement of boating laws. This met the university requirement toward my Criminal Justice Degree and gave me three hours of an A grade. Red Rock is a beautiful lake created by damming the Des Moines River, southeast of Des Moines, for flood control. The lake attracted numerous boaters, fishermen, and campers from central Iowa. The busy days were Friday through Sunday, with Monday our day to complete maintenance on the two patrol boats. The patrol boats consisted of an 18' Bonanza inboard with a straight line six cylinders, 165 HP Mercury engine, and a 19' Sea Sprite with the same engine. They were great boats to drive; the only negative was we had to be in uniform that consisted of long pants and a short sleeve shirt. It was a great job, but we were looked at with a negative attitude by most of the boaters. They were having fun, and we were taking their time away from that fun while we checked them for proper equipment, stopped them for running too fast, or too close to shore.

During slow periods such as Mondays or Thursdays we would accompany the head Waters officers on important missions: fishing, trapping snapping turtles, or arrow head hunting. Any fish or turtles caught were cleaned and placed in a freezer. At the end of the summer session we would have a family get together. Other officers in the area, summer workers, and family would eat up all the summer catch which made for a great time with great food and great people.

A sad note to that summer was the drowning of a young child about five or six years of age. The child was standing in the driver's lap and helping steer the boat. The boat either hit a wave or possibly a submerged log causing both to fall out of the boat. The child was not wearing a life jacket and went under and was lost before anyone could respond. It was almost three days before the body was recovered by relatives who helped in the search.

Another incident occurred after an overnight thunderstorm. Three women came to the office on Monday morning stating their husbands were missing from a fishing trip the day before. The wind and waves were still threatening, but we went on a search and rescue mission. After an hour or so of fighting the waves we slipped into one of the side coves where someone would seek shelter. Sure enough, we came upon three gentlemen who were still well supplied with beverage and food, and they were having a great time story telling. Once we confirmed they were the missing husbands, and that they were all right we headed back to relay the good news to the wives. It's funny how someone can go from extreme worry to being totally pissed off in just a few seconds. In defense of the husbands, they did the right thing to go to shelter and not fight the waves and storm to get back. Those were the days before cell phones so they weren't able to notify anyone of their circumstance. They laid low and made the best of a bad thing.

27

A Girl Named Hope

We were back to school in September of 1974. We still rented on Franklin Street which made it an easy transition into our senior year. All four of us were majoring in Criminal Justice so we helped each other as best we could. Soon an event would change my life, forever. I would meet an angel from Heaven sent to care for me and love me "til death do us part."

The cards were being good to me this night. A poker game was under way at the Lambda House with beer, food, and friends. A telephone call came in for me from Lace's girlfriend. Reluctantly I took the call because it would break the flow of the cards that were in my favor.

Girlfriend: "Mick, I have a sorority sister who needs a date for tonight's Sadie Hawkins Dance." Mick: "you can't find anyone else? I'm in a poker game and I'm winning." GF: "Come on Mick, you'll have a good time. Have I ever set you up wrong?" Come to think of it, I had been very satisfied with some of the girls Lace had introduced me to. "Okay," I said. GF: "We'll pick you up and take you to the Tri Sig dorm."

I was standing by myself next to the fireplace when a pretty little girl went toward Lace. "So, where's my date?" she said to Lace. "He is right over there." I was introduced to a pretty, smiling face. She told me at some point she was five feet tall. I knew she was rounding up to get to five feet, but a very nice five-foot package. Dorothy Aquinata Mary Hope Schlepphorst; "Very pleased to meet you."

For those of you who are not familiar with the tradition of a Sadie Hawkins Dance, the girl is responsible to ask a guy to the dance. Hope had dated a brother of a sorority sister a few times but he was not there this weekend so she was going to stay in the dorm. Somehow, Lace's girlfriend got involved and said "I got a date for you." I'm sure Hope was unsure of a blind date but somehow was convinced she would do her right. I was told later she was very pleased with the tall, good look-ing young man with curly blonde hair down to his shoulders, blue eyes, and a Fu Manchu mustache.

Now this is my side of the story so any interpretation of events will have to come from Hope in her own story. My understanding is she had not eaten much over the previous day or two because the dorm food had caused her to put on some weight. So, Hope had an empty stomach when we reached the party. Not knowing this, of course I got her a cold cup of beer to get things started. It wasn't long into the party that Hope disappeared. She was found in the bathroom sick as a dog. Some of her friends took her outside to walk it off. She sat down in an area used for a skating rink but it was water, no ice. She got out of the water and immediately had to sit down again. This area was more dirt than grass so now her butt was not only wet, but muddy too. Now she was really upset and wanted to go home. So, after a dirty butt cleaning she climbed into the back of Lace's car, a two door sedan. I don't recall much conversation other than "Roll down the window, I have to throw up." Now Lace's car did not have a window that rolled down in the back, so he would stop the car and open the door for Hope to throw up and she would say "Shut the light off!" I'm not sure how many times this happened between Thousand Hills Park and our apartment but we made it. "I'm not going into your apartment. Take me to my dorm." Damn it, the girl still had her wits about her. All I wanted was to clean her up a little that's all. "Take me to my dorm." We talked in the dorm lounge until the early morning hours. I knew this girl was special even with the dramatics of the night before.

Somehow, I was volunteered to let her use my car for a parade or something. Don't need me, just my car. "Yes, I know how to drive a manual transmission." As she drove away I knew she did NOT know how to drive a manual shift. What I did not know was her "I can do it" attitude about any challenge put in front of her. She would try her best at anything and was not afraid to fail. And, in every situation that I am aware of, she has not failed. My Pinto stood the test of her inexperience and was returned in one piece. The good thing was she would later have her own car at school, which saved wear on El Pinto's transmission.

The rest of my story will be somewhat foggy to me because it is being written 41 years since I first met Hope. She has the ability to remember what clothes someone wore during lunch at a pizza parlor 30 years ago. So, as she reads this transcript each night I will be corrected. What I am really worried about is forgetting something she feels was significant and she may be hurt by my omission. I'll apologize now and take some of the edge off her disappointment.

I made a date with Hope to go riding on my motorcycle. She accepted, and we had a nice day of riding around town and out to Thousand Hills State Park. For those that have not been there, it has a lot of hills. It also has a beautiful lake and a nice road for sightseeing. It was in October, so the ducks and geese were passing through Northern Missouri heading south, and used the lake and surrounding fields to rest and feed.

We had a wonderful day together, and we talked and talked; something I was not very good at, especially with a beautiful girl. But, Hope was different; I could talk to her about my past, my family, my brother. I don't remember opening up to her about Vietnam until much later. And something she may not have totally understood until the writing of this manuscript. Not that I didn't want too, but because I saw no reason to go into details, descriptive details. I learned later, that date on the bike ride was not only the beginning of my love for her, but also hers for me.

I asked Hope to be my date for the upcoming homecoming football game and to the Phi Lambda Chi formal dance with actives and alum-ni; she accepted to my relief. I was totally worried I would scare her off by coming on too strong. Hope and some of her Tri Sig friends had been coming to help on the Phi Lambda float for the home coming parade; even without a formal invitation from me. I liked that, and it raised my confidence that she wanted to see me more. Phi Lambda Chi had won the contest for best float in the parade for two or three years; 1974 would be no exception.

It's time I introduced you further to the Phi Lambs of Kirksville, MO. My best description in the past has always been; watch the movie, *Animal House,* and you will understand, and you will also see why I should have been nervous bringing Hope to a formal dance. Up to that point, I had been seen with many girls but not for very long and certainly not to a formal dance. This was a signal to my friends that this girl was special and of course, she was.

Now it's time for me to try to impress Hope with my memory of what she wore to the football game, but I don't. I do remember how much fun we had together and how we laughed at other Phi Lambs in the stands. I am pretty positive that only a small percent were sober and even though we were mixed in with parents and other outstand-ing citizens of the community it did not stop our verbal interactions. F-bombs were dropping as if a B-52 had completed a fly over of the stadium. Someone would see alumni and stand up and shout "Hey, where the fuck you been?" "I don't fucking know you, do I?" And then he would squint as he lifted his drink; "Hey, how the fuck are you? You son of a bitch!" It was plainly marked at the stadium entrance; "No Alcoholic Beverages!" Now that I am a parent, I would be appalled at such behavior, but just for a second.

That night I do remember what Hope wore; a dress. Okay, it was a print dress with cream colors if I remember right. I hope that is close (I am told it was a red dress with white poke-a-dots)—close enough. I know she was beautiful and I know my frat brothers were paying at-tention. As a matter of fact, I didn't like fast dancing unless I was 80% drunk and then only if I really liked the song. But, I did like to slow dance with Hope, even though many times over the years I would stand her on a chair as I held her tight and danced around the chair.

For some reason I was not jealous about others dancing with Hope. Probably because I had matured over the years, and I knew I could trust her. If she found someone she liked more than me, then I know I would have been heartbroken; but there is no use in being jealous about it. Matter of fact, I know I had frat brothers telling her to drop me and date them: brotherly love.

I have nightmares over what happened the next day. It could have become another tragic love story. It was Sunday; the actives were going to play the alumni in a flag football contest. This in itself was a comedy just watching "hung over" bodies run around the field with seriousness on their faces. The contest was taking place at a city park not far from the Lambda House and some of the early arrivals had parked off the street in the grass areas. As Hope and I arrived, we were not aware that a police officer had stopped and was telling people to move their cars to the street. Hope and I were talking and joking with each other. She was probably surprised I was able to function after the drinking of the night before; I don't remember anything past the dinner and dance. But, I am sure Hope will bring it back into focus later. As Hope and I joked around I grabbed her around the neck and playfully took her to the ground. As we laughed and gazed into each other's eyes, a frat brother had started his car and when he looked out the back, could not see us on the ground. As I looked into Hope's eyes I felt pressure on my right knee. As I looked to see what the pressure, now pain, was coming from, my nose was inches from a car's side panel. As the car continued to backup, my knee was 'shot' out from under the tire as the tire fell to the side. I am sure I screamed in pain; Hope probably screamed and others who saw it happen, screamed. My poor frat brother stopped the car and got out to see what happened. He probably almost had a heart attack at a young age when he saw us on the ground. Not his fault, not anyone's fault, it was just something that happened. But it was time to play, so I headed to my team even though I had tread marks across my knee. About three years later I would have knee surgery for a bone spur.

The worst thing about this incident did not happen; Hope and I were lucky the car wasn't a foot to the right because it would have been on top of us with Hope's head at the bottom. As in the previous situations the dreams came back to haunt not only what did happen but even what could have.

•

28

Will You Marry Me

Hope said she was not aware I was scared to ask her out so many times so quick. She had no idea how scared I was to ask the next question. I've told you, I had only been to a couple of county fairs so I sure wasn't aware of the proper way to ask a girl to marry me. I didn't know I should request permission from her father, or to go ahead and buy an engagement ring before asking. I do remember we were alone on the couch on Franklin Street and I somehow had the courage to ask her; "Will you marry me?" Hope said "Yes!" After that I do not remember my response. This all had happened so fast, yet I knew she was the girl I wanted to marry. I had gone the previous four years dating a few girls. I thought I could love some of them, but things would change my feelings or their feelings about me. I had resolved to become a bum for a year and ride my motorcycle all over the US taking in the sites. But, Hope made me forget about all of that. I knew I wanted to spend the rest of my life with her. Little did I know, she wanted to spend her life with me.

Now that I have raised four daughters I can appreciate how upset Hope's parents were when they heard the news from Hope. Her older sister, was also a Tri Sig, a year ahead of Hope, and told Hope I was just using her when Hope told her of our plans. As soon as Hope's dad heard the news, he wanted to know where this guy was from. When told Searsboro, Iowa, he immediately checked an Iowa map. He probably had to go buy one. I told you before, Searsboro was not on most Iowa maps and was not on the one her father looked at. "That son of a bitch has lied to her." Her dad's next thought was to send his youngest brother from Michigan to Missouri to check this guy out. Within a few days Hope's uncle, who was only a few years older than me, was sitting on the couch on Franklin Street; drinking my beer. We had a great conversation. I am sure her dad questioned his own judgment on sending his younger brother and was trying to come up with his next plan of action. Hope had not wanted to go to NEMU to college. She had wanted to stay in Michigan, get a job, and find her future husband, but her dad had pleaded with her to, "Just give it one year to see how you like it." Hope agreed to give college a try, and left just before she turned 18 on October 3rd. What a wonderful idea!

Hope and I began looking around for rings and we also visited her grandparents who lived just down Highway 6, in Edina, MO. They liked me, so I got another yes vote from her grandparents. All of this was going on and I had not mentioned a thing to my parents, I simply told my mom by telephone that I would be coming home with a friend for Thanksgiving. Every friend before had been either Lace or Dan and we would drop off our dirty clothes, grab a meal and then off to Mingo to party. Then back home for a meal, get the clean clothes, a thank you and off to college.

One of the things that I was surprised about was Lace's girlfriend, and her reaction. I found out later she had tried to convince Hope against marrying me. She told Hope everything I had done in four years and who it was done with. Whether it was all true, I don't know. What I know is Hope paid it no mind, and we went on making plans for our wedding date, August 16, 1975.

We went shopping for rings in Kirksville but did not find what Hope wanted. She wanted to wait until she got back to Michigan and I would wire her money needed for the purchase.

Thanksgiving break allowed us to make a trip for Hope to meet my parents even though they did not know she was coming. Dad was traveling and not home yet but mom went nuts. She had probably worried that I would never get married. She was extremely surprised and very happy to see Hope. Mom and Dad were excited when we told them we were getting married. Mom finally would have a daughter.

29

Meeting the Schlepphorst Family

The weather was good on the trip north and I met Hope near the interstate so we could greet each other properly. I was reminded of all her mother's rules; shoes off just outside the door, never put a glass down anywhere on the counter and it goes into the sink when finished; never go into the front living room which was for special events only, it would mess up the carpet; all wet towels must be taken immediately to the wash room. There were more rules but those are the ones that come to mind. I remember them because I made it a point to break all of them. When introduced, and the pleasantries were made, I headed toward the kitchen, shoes and all. I was asked to take my shoes off by Hope's mom, and I obliged. What rule can I break next? But, her parents and I got along great. Her dad had since found a map with Searsboro on it. Because her mom worked at Sears, they felt I had made the place up and was planning to run off with Hope. They were right on that part; we would run off later that spring when I visited after my graduation and before I started my summer job again with the Conservation Commission. One of my cousin's from Dads side, Steve Smith was getting married to Janie Pyle and Hope wanted to come back to Iowa for the wedding. She would drive her car and follow me but her parents wanted her to stay home. Her folks were upset but Hope followed me home to my parents.

Hope and I attended Steve and Janie's wedding; I was one of the groomsmen. Hope and I went with Steve and Janie on part of their honeymoon, to Omaha, for the AKSARBEN (Nebraska spelled backward) horse races. Steve knew a man in Newton, IA who owned racehorses and ran them on the AKSARBEN circuit of racetracks around Nebraska. Steve and I met with the man and listened to the morning radio program that announced the number of races, what horses were in each race, and what the weather and track conditions would be. Out of eleven races for the day, the man told us to only place bets on nine of them. The reason not to bet on two races was because one owner had multiple horses in each race and any one of them might win. This made the odds not worth the bet. We owe that man our gratitude.

Once at the track, we sat outside for the first two to three races. It was very hot that day, but we were having a great time. Later we would discover a large inside auditorium; air conditioned, cold beer close by, and a large screen to view the races. Out of the nine races we placed bets on, we won in seven of those races. Steve and I would sit and watch the races drinking a nice cold beer. Hope and Janie would run up to the window to get our winnings and then place bets for the next race; all pre-planned by our meeting in Newton. People sitting around us were starting to get curious about our success. With one last race to go a man asked who we were betting on. We gave him our picks, and the bets were made. That was one of the two races we lost. I am sure the man was pissed. Hope and I had a budget set at $25 for the race bets with a little more to have to eat and share gas money. Because of this we were only betting $2 tickets to win place or show. I believe we won over $75 on that second race alone. The man had told us this second race was the best to buy an "exacta ticket" for $10 for the first and second place finish. That would have been almost half our money on one race so we bet the $2 ticket on each horse. It was a photo finish with the horses finishing exactly like the owner had said; the exacta ticket was close to $1,000. Oh well, we had a great time anyway, drank beer all day, had a steak dinner on the way home, and money in our pocket when we got home.

MEETING THE SCHLEPPHORST FAMILY

Hope's mom and sister came to Iowa that summer for a wedding shower my mom put on for our side of the family. Also, Hope and I spent a weekend camping at Red Rock with Steve and Janie, Calvin and Beth, and other friends from Newton. The bummer was I had to work on the lake during the day as the Water Patrol while everyone else was having a good time. But, I made the best of it after work. Don't come knocking when the tents are rocking.

30

The Wedding

Our wedding was on schedule and we both could not wait. I was able to wire money to Hope to purchase the rings. She found what we could afford but her dad continued to doubt if I would send any money. Hope's only problem was getting the marriage license because they refused to believe my given name was Mickey. "You mean he is called Mickey but his real name is Michael." "No, his real name is MICKEY." After asking over and over, Hope's father said; "you have asked and she has answered it; now make out the license." My parents could not remember exactly whose choice it was to name me Mickey, but it was for Mickey Mouse, Mickey Rooney, or Mickey Mantle. I always chose Mickey Mantle as my namesake. Not long ago I learned about generation gaps when girls working at the golf course I worked at, were asking me about my name. I told them about the three choices but the only one they knew was Mickey Mouse. I told them Mickey Rooney was an actor, but they did not know him. "You know, he was in a lot of movies with Elizabeth Taylor." "Who is she?" they responded. No need to even mention Mickey Mantle.

Hope was able to get the license and continued to plan with her parents. They wanted the reception to be special, and they wanted a live band, not the typical DJ used today. They watched the wedding announcements in the paper and started going to receptions and clubs to find the right band; they succeeded.

Craig Jackson and I were working the Water Officer positions at Red Rock and he was not able to get off for the wedding. Lace, Dan, and Sam Owens (my frat little brother) were flown in by Dan's father, James McCabe. Mr. McCabe was a welcome addition because he is simply a great man with a wonderful sense of humor. The McCabe's are Catholic and most Catholics I know are not against having a beer or two or more. At one point during the weekend James was riding with my friends from Mingo and had them convinced he was a Baptist Minister and he did not appreciate the alcohol being consumed or the language being used in his presence. Then he said "What the hell, give me a beer," or something to that effect.

The wedding groomsmen consisted of Steve Smith "Smitty" as my best man. My brother was in the Air Force and not sure if he would be able to attend, but he did make it. Dan and Lace finished out the groomsman. Hope's sister, was the maid of honor and the rest were her cousin Denise Dickey (Wilcox-Terryah), Tammy Brow (Blazer), and Lisa Slezsak.

We had a great pre-wedding dinner at Italian Gardens, where the favorite meal was spaghetti and spatini, which is steak and onion sauté. Good friends from Mingo drove to the wedding, including Harold Perry, Bill and Paula Maher, Ed Doty, and others. Mom and dad, mom's brother and his wife, mom's parents, Harvey and Gertrude Teed (Nanny and Popeye) also attended. My grandfather was called Popeye because he looked like him; not much hair, small in stature, but arms bigger than someone his size.

Bob and Jim Gannon were coming from NY with Jim's wife to be, Angela. The timing for them to stop in Michigan was perfect. We found out later they had stopped at the hotel Hope and I had chosen for our wedding night. During the discussion, the clerk inadvertently mentioned that Hope and I had a room reservation. This could have been a bad thing but people had so much fun at the reception they did not want to leave; or were unable to drive.

The wedding went perfect. Hope and I left in her maroon Buick LeSabre that would have stains on it forever from shave cream, used to wish us well and to make other comments normally used for that occasion.

Off to the reception and dinner all in Flushing, MI, at the VFW Hall. There was plenty of great food and drinks for all. The band took over and made it a reception/dance still talked about today. They were great musicians but more than that, they got everyone involved. When Hope and I left by midnight they were still going strong. Lace, Dan and the others were in the parking lot as we took off. Lace had just fallen off a vehicle onto a recently repaved asphalt parking lot in his white tuxedo. When I gathered the tuxes up the next day, I made sure his was in the bottom of the return bag. Hope and I changed hotels for one more night, then the rest of our honeymoon consisted of the drive back to Iowa; I was due back at work on Wednesday. Along the way, we had our first dinner together at a restaurant just off the Tipton, IA exit. Hope had lobster, her favorite meal, with many more to come.

Hope and I had saved as much money as we could to keep us going until I had a full-time job. With our saving's, and the generosity of wedding cash from family and friends, we would be okay for a while. We would stay with mom and dad until we knew the direction our lives would take. I was due to have an interview for a Park Ranger position and Water's Officer, which was opening up in September. I was not offered a position with the Park Service but Craig Jackson was interviewed and offered an assistant position. This would lead to a lifetime career with Craig and the Iowa DNR.

31

My Career

My interview for the waters officer position was coming up, but the consensus was another summer worker had more experience and was expected to get the vote. The process came down to the interview in front of a dozen members of the department. Three of us made it to the interview, and we were brought in, one at a time, and stood at attention while questions were asked from around the table. After all three of us were interviewed, it came down to a vote by each member of the department. They were to vote for first, second, and third place choice to determine who was hired. The vote came down to me and the front-runner, we tied for first place votes. One of the supervisors voted for his candidate, the third person, in first place and me in second place. I won the position with one more second place vote.

Hope and I packed what little we had and drove both our vehicles to Guttenberg, IA; a beautiful little town on the Mississippi River in Northeast Iowa. My office was in the fish hatchery on the river in the middle of town. Main Street ran along the river with a lock, dam, and hatchery on one side, and business locations across from the river. Because this was a new position, there were no Waters Officer Residence or support buildings for the office and boat storage. They were planned for the future, but for then, Hope and I had to look for a place to live. We found the perfect apartment right on Main Street above the insurance office. It was just two blocks from the hatchery and across from the lock and dam. It had three bedrooms, a large kitchen, dining area, and living room. It was more space than we needed and was more or less furnished. We had a laundry room and our first purchase was a washer and dryer: how romantic. Hope enjoyed the large bathroom where she could set up her sewing machine. She enjoyed making her own clothes and made some shirts for me on occasion. We still joke to each other because of some flannel shirts she started for me about a year into our marriage. She wanted to measure my arm for the sleeve length but I was too busy or something. After asking me several times and not getting the measurements, she put the main part of the shirts away and has refused to complete them. By now, they would not fit my frame any more anyway.

We enjoyed our time in Guttenberg. It was going into fall colors and the Mississippi back waters provided a beautiful ride on the river. I enjoyed working the river as the weather turned cooler. The duck season went into full gear and I was able to work with the Federal Game agents to help check people for licenses and to check the types of ducks and geese taken. One morning we headed out in darkness in a canoe with a small motor. This allowed us to make our way deep into the hunting areas. By daylight, I was totally lost and would have no way of finding my way back to the trucks alone.

A day off allowed Hope and I to visit areas along the river; where we found good people and great restaurants. A great day trip was into Wisconsin and a visit to the House on the Rock. This home wrapped around the boulders and trees with little interruptions of nature. The home and adjacent buildings are a Regional Tourist Attraction, and a must visit site for anyone who goes to Wisconsin to see fall colors or any time of the year.

Hope and I discussed our plans for children and decided to wait a couple of years to allow us to get settled in financially. What we didn't realize is that God knows when and where children will come. Forget about being financially settled. Hope came home from a doctor's appointment and asked me to go into the bathroom because our landlord was working on the apartment or something. Hope had changed the type of birth control pill after moving to Guttenberg and her doctor declared her pregnant. What wonderful news and we celebrated the coming of our first child.

One of my counterparts on the Missouri River had decided to take a job with the Idaho DNR and this left an opening for Water's Officer at Wilson Island. I was contacted by the Supervisor for the West Region. The position's salary was the same but it would give us state housing, eliminating our rent cost. We made the move to Wilson Island recreation area near Missouri Valley, IA, in early spring of 1976. We had saved some money but this would go to our purchase of furniture since we had lived in a furnished apartment. Wilson Island was a 500-acre island along the Missouri River just south of the Federal Wildlife area called De Soto Bend. This was a major flyway for the annual migration of the ducks and geese and a popular hunting area. I purchased a German Short-Hair hunting dog and named him Duke. He was young and anxious to learn and we had some good hunting together. Duke joined in on the first day with Dotenhagen, a miniature Dachshund. Hope had picked up Dote as a runt pup while we were at college. The pair of Dote and Duke was a real Mutt and Jeff. Whenever the two would hunt in the fields around home, Dote had to bounce up and down in the tall grass to see where she was going.

For a time, Hope and I were on the island with a part-time employee but were later joined by a young Park Ranger and his wife, Mike and Donna Schoneboom. The Ranger complex had an area with bunks and showers for seasonal help to stay or guests to stay on hunting trips. Craig Jackson and some other Conservation personnel came to stay during goose season. With an estimated 250,000 geese moving through the area it made for an easy hunt. All five of us had our limit of five geese probably within an hour. Duke was confused why I had stopped shooting and stared at me, then would look up at the geese going over head just tree top high. He probably thought I was taking his fun of fetching away from him for some reason. I tried to explain we had our limit, but he wanted more. I am sure he was thinking; "dumb ass."

One time, my cousin Smitty and his friend Calvin Simbro came to hunt ducks and geese. I took them into De Soto Bend just to look at the geese passing through. In one large open area there were thousands of snow geese so thick it looked like snow on the ground. Something, possibly a coyote, spooked the geese and they all came up and over my truck as they took flight. Their honking was so loud you could hardly hear the loud yells from Smitty and Calvin as goose shit rained down on the truck.

De Soto Bend was over 2600 acres of wild life preserve with an oxbow lake in the middle. The lake was the old river bed which had been isolated just before WWII when the Army Corps of Engineers were re-routing the river to improve the ability of barges to transport commodities up and down the river. It was a perfect oasis for wildlife with timber, crop fields, and water. Local farmers were allowed to plant crops such as corn then a percentage of the crop was left standing for wildlife to feed on. I took my father on a tour of the area once just before dark. He lost track after counting over 300 deer as we passed open fields where they began to graze.

The confusing part of the Missouri River at the time was the legal battle between Nebraska and Iowa over the state boundaries. The river, as it was then, would normally be considered the State line running down the center. The States had agreed that once the Army Corps of Engineers completed the work on channeling the river that would be the border. But, WWII took the Corp away from their work and the river made its own changes during the war. What a mess of litigation this caused. I am sure a generation or two of attorneys have made their living fighting this battle in court. My boss had grown up on the river and was used as an expert witness over the years. He was a large man with a booming voice, known as the "Bull of the woods." He was a good boss in that he told you what he wanted and trusted you would get it done. He liked to grow tomatoes and had a huge area planted in tomatoes on the island. I did work, but it was more fun than work. I've seen as many as 20 bald eagles in a tree along the river and would take the boat up river turn it off then float past them to get a "bird's-eye view." I know that was bad, but I just had to say it. I've taken Hope for rides through De Soto Bend to see the wild life; bald eagles, deer, ducks and geese, fox, coyote, and possum. Hope had a run in with a possum one day when Dote and Duke started raising a fuss in the yard. A possum, normally nocturnal, was in the yard ready to fight. Hope grabbed my 12 gauge shot gun, got the dogs clear and blew away the possum. I forgot to tell you how scared I am of Hope and that is one reason. The other reason is; when we watched a movie just a few months after we were married. The movie was, *The Burning Bed*, with Farah Faucet. The movie depicts a physically abused housewife who was on trial for murder. One night after she had been beaten her husband fell asleep, in a drunken stupor. The woman douses him and the bed with gas and lights it up. Hope never said a word; just looked at me with eyes that said, "Don't mess with me or something like that could happen to you." It has been yes madam, no madam ever since.

32

Dangerous River

With all the positive and good things about the river, there was a negative side. The river had become so channelized that the river current was fast and dangerous, whirlpools were created around dikes built to protect the riverbanks from erosion. These pools were extremely dangerous and one near the campground took the life of two young boys, one twelve and the other a year or two older. The younger one fell into the current and the other boy tried to save him. Both drowned in the same spot but were later found over 30 miles apart. After searching with nets and divers without success it would be a matter of waiting until the gasses build up and the body comes to the top. Three days later a radio transmission from a tugboat and barge south of Omaha reported finding the older and larger of the boys. Two Nebraska Game Wardens were assisting in the search and I joined them to look for the younger boy.

A radio transmission alerted us that two ladies fishing north of Omaha and just south of Wilson Island had seen the boy come up near their boat, but the body would later go back under as the stream carried it toward Omaha. We spotted the boy numerous times, but then we would lose site as he sunk before we could reach him. Then as I stared into the muddy water he came up within reach of the boat, and I grabbed one of his arms waiting for the body bag to be readied.

The boy's family had been listening to the radio transmissions and his mother met me as I came off the boat dock. She thanked me for finding her son. I asked her to wait until later to see her son, hoping the coroner could try to make him look like the son she lost; but I knew that could not be done.

Later that year another young teenager drowned while crossing the river at night. He was unable to see the barge tied along the bank and his boat was taken under the barge by the swift current. The third morning, one of my summer employees and I launched the boat and started north toward the area where he drowned. It was early morning with a little wind and fog skimming the river, we saw him within a mile or so from our starting point. I had my employee steer the boat while I worked to secure the body with a rope around the waist and through the legs. We did not have a boat with the rear landing to secure the body to, so we worked our way toward a small inlet to get away from the current. We did not have a body bag, so I tied the rope to a tree limb, and then we moved the boat upwind away from the body. As we sat waiting for the Nebraska personnel to arrive, we heard someone walking through the woods. A man who appeared to be in his twenties was hiking, walked up to the tree, and looked down at the body. He did not see us and when I said, "Go away" he turned and ran as fast as he could. I am sure he had to change himself when he got back home. The Douglas County Sheriff's Patrol arrived with a body bag and recovered the boy's body.

33

Mandy

Early in July of 1976 Hope was nearing delivery of a girl. Hope had a rough pregnancy in that she became allergic to the baby and broke out in hives. During the hot month of June she only wore a sheet wrapped around her. This was embarrassing when we went grocery shopping and to church. OK, she wore clothes then. Our concern also was the nearest hospital was about 40 miles away in Council Bluffs. As we neared her due date, it looked like we had a chance to have a Bi-Centennial baby. The doctor told us it could be any day, so I started working her hard, running over rough roads, rail road tracks, and had her scrubbing the bath tub. But, July 4th came and went so I relaxed and figured she would go a few more days. About 5am the next morning Hope woke me stating her water had broken. We had been taking Lamaze classes, so I was calm and cool getting ready to head out, NOT.

We made the trip in fine time and even made a tape recording on the way to the hospital. At the hospital, we all settled in waiting for the baby. We did not know the baby's sex but each nurse that would check Hope would say "That's a boy's heart beat." "No, doubt about it, that is a boy." When Mandy finally got her head out, I could hear her say "I don't have a penis!" Mandy Mary Mae was born at 11:13 am, July 5, 1976. Mandy was picked because of Barry Manilow's popular song. She was a beautiful baby with lots of black hair. Just days before Smitty and Janie had their first baby, Jeremy. As the time neared for their first birthday, Smitty, Janie, and Jeremy came to Wilson Island to celebrate the kids first birthdays. Each had their own little cake to eat, smear, and throw around at each other. While they were there, I received a call about 2:00am from the Nebraska Sheriff's Department asking for assistance. Two men were reported in trouble on the river. Smitty rode with me as we worked our way up river in fog so thick we could barely see the shoreline. About five miles up we came upon a boat inside a small inlet but with only one man. The man explained that he had run out of gas and he and his friend started arguing. The other man took off his clothes and jumped overboard about two hours before. As we were talking to the man in the boat, the other man swam up to the boat. He had been swimming trying to catch up to the boat but could never catch up because of the current speed. He also had floated past a marina and restaurant but didn't go ashore because he had nothing on but underwear. The men still wanted to fight, but we were able to get them separated and taken to the marina where a Sheriff's Deputy waited to pick them up. Both men were lucky they had not run into a barge along the way.

Mandy was talking and walking at an early age and I began to have night mares that she would somehow get out of the house and down to the river. The vision of a floater is not something you want to see much less think it would be your child. I began to have second thoughts regarding a career in conservation work. I saw officers getting ready to retire, but they were still planning to get another job to make payments on a home. They had lived in State housing all their career and now had to buy a home for somewhere to live. I started watching ads for jobs and considered applying for the Omaha Police Department. Then I ran across a sales job with Jewel T Company out of Chicago. They provided a delivery service to homes from everything like boxed foods, pillows, clothes, and all types of items for the home. It was a Wal-mart on wheels.

34

Career Change

I resigned from the State job February 1978 and Hope, Mandy, and I moved to an apartment in a suburb of Omaha. I was given a delivery truck, a route of customers and a storage facility of stock items. We could not have a pet in the apartments so my grandparents, Nanny and Popeye, agreed to keep the dog until we could find a home. Duke had to be destroyed the winter before when he became sick during an extremely cold spell. I had gone into the hospital to have a bone spur removed from my knee that was run over by the car in 1975. One vet misdiagnosed Duke with hookworm, and another vet found he had heart worm. He was too weak from the medication and had to be put down when his kidneys failed. Hope and I had spent over $200 on him, which was almost all our savings at the time.

Once we moved to Omaha, Hope got a job waiting tables while I started building my route customers. I enjoyed working for Jewell T. I was able to meet and work with great customers and was rookie of the month my first few months. The biggest problem was trying to find customers who could afford the service. Too many customers lived off welfare and were tough to find toward the end of the month. I met each customer every two weeks. They could purchase items I had on the truck or order from the catalog. I collected for items I delivered and took orders for the next trip. I became discouraged trying to collect from customers who would not answer the door, or they would have their children lie saying their parents weren't home. Looking back on this I can see where some women would not put up with a husband like me. Decide what you want and stick with it.

I finally decided Jewell T was not for me about six months into the job. Hope and I made our way back to the Grinnell, IA area where I took a construction job with my uncle. We lived in the county in an old farm house that was nice enough but had some flaws; such as cracks in the foundation big enough that ground squirrels were seen running through the master bedroom. There was a small bedroom for Mandy upstairs that was more like a ladder than stairs. But we enjoyed the country and were now close to mom and dad and just two and one half hours to Hope's parents, who had moved to Kirksville, Missouri after her father retired from General Motors. After working with my uncle a few months I had the opportunity to work for an electrician. What he did not tell me was that he planned to sell his business within a few months. My mom's youngest brother was in Grinnell working as an engineer for GTE/MW. He asked me about working as a lineman, and once in the company I would have the education and experience for a security investigator position. My uncle made the contacts to get me an interview, and I was offered a job as a lineman in Nevada, IA., just about 40 miles from Grinnell. We still could not afford to purchase a home yet but the job paid more than my State jobs without figuring any overtime. 1978 was a crazy year with moves form Missouri Valley, to Omaha, to Grinnell, and then to Nevada.

Once on the job it was winter time and most of the line work consisted of wrecking out old wire lines and pulling poles. It was hard work, but I enjoyed being outside and got along with my counterparts. Hope and I had moved into an apartment/duplex with hopes of finding a home.

Within a few months we found what the other residents called "The Cottage." It was in our price range; with help from the VA, we could get the loan with no down payment. It was a three bedroom, one story, with laundry facilities in the basement and storage in the attic.

Our first home cost us $47,500.00; less than most luxury cars of today. But it was our first home and with Hope's ability to decorate; it was one we were proud of. She even made all the window curtains to save money. We painted the house a light yellow to satisfy the loan requirements but other than that there were no major issues with the house.

35

Mary Elizabeth "Buffy"

Hope was hired by Donnelly Marketing and we were making enough money to stay comfortable. That fall of 1979 we had another baby on the way. We were only four blocks away from the hospital so no sweat we thought. On November 19th Hope's water broke, and I didn't think we were going to make it in time. Hope already wanted to push as we met the first nurse. The nurses said she wasn't dilated enough; but go ahead and push. When Hope pushed she maxed out immediately, and the surprised nurse called for the doctor. When he arrived and checked Hope he said it would be awhile. He would go lay down in the doctor's lounge. The doctor had not gotten to the end of the hall when Hope pushed again and the baby's crown was exposed. The nurse yelled for the doctor.

The baby was coming and Hope hadn't had a shot yet to numb the area for the episiotomy. The doctor went ahead and cut her to give the baby more room. Hope's eyes lit up like electric lights and she damn near broke my hand. "You bastard!" she screamed. I think she was yelling at the doctor, not me. According to the nurses this was a boy for sure. The heart beat and other signs made them certain it was a boy. But, when Mary Elizabeth Schlepphorst Thomas got her head out, I heard her say; "I don't have a penis!" Then out she came; I nicknamed her "Buffy."

The doctor checked Hope and found her bleeding internally from a tear caused by the speed of the delivery. As he sewed her up inside and out I slipped him an extra twenty dollars for one more stitch. Okay, okay; it's a guy thing.

I need to fill in some family history on Hope's mother's side. As far back as anyone remembers, if the mother was named Mary, the second daughter was named Dorothy; then her second daughter was named Mary, and down the line. We did not find out until after naming our second daughter, Mary Elizabeth, that Hope's great grandmother Mary was also Mary Elizabeth. Now we had two beautiful girls just like their mother. But, we were just six months away from an event that would put a huge strain on our marriage. If not for Hope's strength it could have been a sad end to our love for each other: at least her love for me.

36

Rescued by Angels

It was May, 1980; Joe, the lead lineman, and myself, were sent out somewhere between Nevada and Ames, Iowa, to wreck out an old two wire line that ran back to a farm residence. I dropped Joe at the beginning of the line and he would climb from pole to pole dropping the wire until he would reach the truck where I dropped it off. I started to climb where the lines went over railroad signal wires at a railroad crossing. I grabbed the first pole and shook; it felt solid. I climbed to the top, about 20 feet, and just wrapped one leg around the pole, rather than buckling my safety strap. The pole was leaning out over the ditch which was about ten feet below the gravel road. I went to the top side, so I was looking toward the road and toward the direction the pole was leaning. I attempted to loosen the double weather wrap holding the wires to the insulators but was unable to budge it. I felt the pole was strong enough, and I wanted to keep the telephone wires out of the barbed wire fence directly below me; a costly mistake. As I cut the second wire the jolt to the pole snapped it. What I had not realized was the pole was rotten below the ground with just a few inches of the core intact. As I felt the pole snap the hair on my neck stood up and I had the feeling this was it for me; I won't survive this fall. I actually had the question flash through my mind; I made it through Vietnam to die on this fucking pole? As the pole started down I knew I had to stay with it until I could balance and attempt to jump away as it hit the ground. If I didn't the pole would bounce off the ground with enough force to crush whatever part of me it hit. My thoughts and decision took all of two seconds before I jumped away to the left and smashed into the bottom of the ditch. The fact I had not buckled to the pole saved my life. The top of the pole shattered on impact. My left leg took the majority of the blow and the steel shank of my climbers transferred the force up my leg, shearing off the tibia plateau in my knee. My left hip, back and head came next, with the force of the contact throwing my hard hat up and out of the 10 foot ditch, across the road, and into the opposite ditch. The wind was knocked out of me and I fought to get air. If you ever had the breath knocked out of you, you understand the feeling that you might not breathe again. I did not lose consciousness, but was stunned and I began slipping into shock; not fully aware of what happened next.

Out of nowhere, there appeared someone putting a blanket over my body. The person was behind me so I never actually saw them. Joe was a smoker, and I thought he would pass out after running the half-mile or so in the steel climbers he wore. It took him a while before he could say anything. Two women in a car had stopped as they witnessed my fall; one got two army blankets out of the car to cover me while the other lady drove to the nearest farmhouse to call for an ambulance. The women stayed with me and Joe until the rescue personnel came, then they disappeared in the confusion. Because of the steepness of the ditch, it took everything the men had to lift me out and into the ambulance.

Joe said he looked up at one point and the Volkswagen bug and women were gone. I don't know if I thanked them or not but they were never identified. My supervisor and rescue personnel never found out who they were or where they came from. What I do know is they were there to help me survive. I was taken to an Ames, IA hospital in serious but stable condition. I remained conscious while x-rays were taken and the surgery team prepared to operate. While waiting after x-rays I asked for a cigarette and was told smoking was not allowed in

the rooms. "So take me out into the hallway." "Sir, we can't do that."
I must have been blunt with my next request because I was lying on a
gurney in the hallway, smoking a cigarette, when Hope came in. She
had not been given much information when the construction secretary
called, because they did not know much other than I had an accident
and was taken to the hospital.

Hope had heard this just a year before when I had to be taken to
the Nevada, IA Hospital. I had sliced open my left thigh while using a
hook knife while trying to strip a support cable for an aerial telephone
cable. I was on a pole and had to climb down on my own because the
technician working in the bucket next to me about passed out. He was
able to recover and drive me to the hospital where it took the doctors
nine stitches to close the thigh muscle and eleven more to close the
skin. Obviously, I was not helping GTE Telephone and their safety
record.

Shortly after Hope's arrival, I was taken into surgery and had three
threaded pins inserted through my tibia plateau, and held in place on
both sides of my knee with regular nuts you could buy at a hardware
store. I was put on morphine after surgery, then Demerol, and then
weaned down to Percocet before leaving the hospital a few days later.
After having morphine, I can understand how people become addicted
to drugs such as heroin and cocaine. You feel indestructible and good
enough to allow someone to cut off fingers or toes just to get more.
The doctors had not found anything else broken, but I had pulled
muscles, tendons and ligaments that would have to heal over time. An
MRI was not available back then, or they would have discovered I had
half a brain; but Hope already knew that. I don't remember much else
about the hospital visit but I am sure the nurses celebrated the day I
left. All I remember was they were not going to let me go home until
I had urinated. When this had not happened by their schedule a male
nurse was sent in to catheterize me; he must have been trying to stick
a ½ inch line into a ¼ inch hole, because it wasn't working; and I was
tired of him trying. When he left to get help, I got out of bed and made
it to the bathroom on my own at which time urination had arrived.

I have the vivid memory of getting home from the hospital because my night would continue well into the morning hours and for reasons not having anything to do with my condition. Hope's parents and my folks shared in staying and taking care of Buffy and Mandy while Hope visited the hospital. Hope's parents left the day I returned home. That evening, I settled back into my EZ Boy to pass the night. I could not lie down in bed because my cast went from my toes to my butt with my knee slightly bent and my toes pointed. Hope has about to learn what the hospital nurses already knew; I was a big baby; worse than Mandy or Buffy. As I started to fall asleep, with help from my drugs, I was startled awake with blood curdling screams coming from the bedroom. Hope continued screaming as I got to my feet and crutches; thinking she was being attacked. When I turned on the light I could see she had the covers over her head. She screamed that there was a bat in the room and refused to get out of bed to help me shut the doors into Mandy's room and Buffy's nursery. When I got back to Hope and turned out the light, the bat flew out of the bedroom and into the main part of the house.

We determined later that Hope's father had gone into the attic during the day because their dog would continue to stand at the door and bark. The door into the attic was in our bedroom and the bat must have flown into the bedroom when the door was left open while he checked out the attic.

Meantime, we will get back to the bat. I shut the bedroom door and turned on the lights to see where the bat went. As the lights came on, I saw the bat fly into the front porch area that had a ceiling of about 12 feet. The bat was perched up into the highest corner and I could not reach him with my crutch. When I turned the lights off the bat started circling the open floor plan from the dining room, living room, and into the front porch and continued circling around looking for a way out. At some point, out of frustration, I swung at the bat with a crutch. I lost my balance and all of my weight went onto my broken leg to keep from falling. My weight crushed the cast onto my toes and they were turning blue as I went into the bedroom to ask Hope for help.

"Shut the door!" she yelled, still under the blankets. "I closed the damn door; now pull this cast off my toes!"

Before going further, I should regress to the point when Hope's scream woke the dead. She had gone to bed after putting her "three" babies to bed. When she got in bed she started to hear a swishing sound. She got up to turn on the light, nothing, no sound; light off, back to bed. The swishing sound began again and this time the bat landed on the pillow next to her head; thus, the blood curdling screams.

Back to the bat; I'm suffering because my toes hurt from being smashed. The bat keeps flying in circles while I try to figure out how to get it outside. At around 2:00am I gave up. I called the non-emergency number for the police and explained my situation; they sent an officer to the house. With the lights on, the bat would land up in the corner of the porch ceiling. I handed a crutch to the officer; he steps up on a small ledge, reaches up and smashes the bat. Out goes the officer with the bat for evidence within a minute.

The next day, Hope is at work and notices some of her girls talking and laughing among each other. As supervisor of a large group of people she went over and asked what the fun was all about. One of the girls said "You won't believe this! My husband is a police officer, and he was called to a house to help a man with a broken leg and a hysterical wife. He killed a bat that was flying around the house. Can you believe that?" as they laughed they noticed Hope was not. "That was me and my husband you're talking about." They stopped laughing and scattered back to work.

The first two weeks at home was miserable while I tried to get used to the cast and not being able to sleep in bed. Also, I had damaged almost every muscle in my body and I was like a rubber band stretched to the max; unable to release the tension. I finally called my supervisor one day and asked him to take me to the doctor. I was given muscle relaxers and that helped a great deal.

The next three months was a terrible ordeal for Hope. I was almost helpless the first few weeks, unable to care for the kids or help around the house. Hope was working six days a week at Donnelly Marketing

and only had Sundays to deal with shopping, meals, laundry, and the worst part, mowing the lawn. We had a large yard with many bushes and trees, and with Hope's size; it was hard for her to push the mower. She would have to stop to check on me and the girls with no time for herself. She has often said she hated me during that time. Most women would not have been able to handle it but Hope is not ordinary in any way. She even complained of always having to be on top; I'm not sure what she was referring to.

Within a month of my accident, I received a call from the Security Director for the Midwest group of GTE. He and his investigator came to Nevada and took me to lunch. It was the first time I had ventured out of the house other than to the doctor. We had a good talk about my previous experience, and he let me know he would be looking for me to fill the next opening in the department.

By August, I was well enough to take on light duty tasks and went back to work. My doctor had judged my knee to be about 80% and would never be back to 100%. Unknown to Hope and me, this evaluation equaled to over $6,000 in a worker's comp payment. This was an unexpected bonus for us and it came at just the right time. We bought a used Chevy Impala and Hope's Dining Room set. I was contacted in October by the Security Director, who wanted me to come to Grinnell for an investigator position. What a thrill for both of us. We could be closer to both sets of parents and no more climbing poles for me. The increase in salary was almost double what I made as a lineman. We were starting to feel comfortable with our income and less stress over making the dollars stretch to the end of the month. The negative was taking Hope away from her job. They had plans to move Hope higher because she was smart, pretty, had a great sense of humor, and people liked working for her. But, Grinnell was too far to commute to Nevada and Hope would start anew.

A benefit we had during the move to Grinnell was the use of a company apartment directly across the street from work. We were allowed to live there while looking for a home. As it turned out, we were allowed to live in the apartment for almost three months while we remodeled an older home on Spencer Street, just three blocks from the office. Hope and I looked at most everything available in the price we could afford. But, could not find what we were looking for. Many of the homes were old, two stories with large porches and beautiful open stairs in the entry foyer. But, they were beyond what we could afford. We had not been in the Nevada home long enough so we had very little equity. But GTE had a moving package that included the purchase of our home after so many weeks on the market.

One day Hope and I looked at an old two story house on Spencer Street. It was the home of the neighbors, Arlene and Bill. They moved next door into a single story brick home where Arlene's mother lived until she passed away. The old two-story house was not in very good shape and needed a lot of work. But, the price was right. I met with my uncle that had a construction business to get an estimate to re-shingle the roof, rewire, remodel the kitchen, add a large addition to the back for an entry, add a laundry room and large bathroom, repaint inside and out, and re-carpet upstairs and downstairs. When I told Hope this would be our new home she sat down on the steps and cried. She could not envision how the home would look once completed. I knew she would be happy once it was finished, and the company allowed us to stay in the apartment until the house was finished. A lot of work to be done, but with me helping on the weekends it started to take shape in no time. We were also able to add a deck on the back so we could enjoy the shade of large oak trees. The lot was not very wide, but it was exceptionally deep at almost 300-feet. We had mature flowering bushes, grape vines, and a beautiful garden area. The garden was actually in both ours and Bill and Arlene's yard because of it being her mother's property. We had lots of planting area and Hope enjoyed having her own garden for fresh vegetables and sweet corn.

The home was finally ready and I know Hope was totally surprised how we had transformed the home and brought it up to date with the addition and kitchen over-haul. Gone were the ugly metal cupboards, rusted out sink cabinet, and the linoleum with metal strips. We now had a nice laundry area just off the kitchen with a large closet for hanging coats and hiding boots, shoes, etc… The deck was nicely done, and made a nice transition from the stand alone two-car garage.

Now that we had the dining room Hope was able to purchase a Thomasville dining set that we still have today. Her Buick was finally wearing out and my pinto was long sold off. We picked up a nice used Chevy Caprice with low mileage. Things were going good, and the job kept me busy with travel. The nice thing was the five-minute walking commute to work. Little did I know how special this was until it was gone.

Bill and Arlene were wonderful neighbors and I know Arlene was excited to see the changes made to her old home. Bill was a character and liked his drink. He was one of the most decorated Iowan's from WWII. He was wounded several times and I'm sure the drink dulled the memories and some of his pain. He loved Mandy and Buffy, and would take them on walking adventures around the neighborhood. Everybody loved Bill and Arlene; she worked in the local restaurant inside the drugstore.

Sometime in 1981-1983, I had an episode at home, later called a panic attack. This happened after a long hot week with travel to Nebraska. Upon arriving home, to the house which did not have central air, the temperatures during that week were in the range of 110-118, I was watching TV while the girls were playing on the floor. My memory of the event is hard to recall because I lost any sense of balance and logical thought. My mind was racing, and I was over the top with panic. I told Hope I thought she was going to shoot me. I believe she ran the girls next door then somehow got me into the car and to the hospital. I spent the night in the hospital and the panic subsided sometime late that night. I was totally fine the next morning when the doctor came in. My blood work and urine found no drugs or anything out of the normal. The doctor started to insinuate one of us was having an affair and I reacted emotionally to the situation. This was totally off base and Hope called her Uncle, a Doctor of Osteopathy in Missouri. Because I was a veteran, her uncle made contact with the VA and set and appointment for me to see a VA Psychiatrist in Iowa City. At the

VA Medical Center they gave me about every test possible to include a CAT-Scan of my brain. They found nothing! I mean they found my brain but saw nothing wrong.

I then sat thru questioning by the Psychiatrist with Hope in the room with me. The lady doctor asked me to name any events where I had head trauma, so I started with the pole accident and worked my way down the line. After the following stories they were both laughing until tears came.

"Well, I had the pole accident, (which I mentioned earlier) then I probably got knocked out once or twice during football. There was the time in basketball my senior year that I was knocked out, and my nose was broken when I came down on top of a guy's head. Then there was the time I was playing tag in the haymow and I was on top of the hay about 8-10 feet above the hardwood floor. I peeked over the edge and saw my Uncle looking around the corner. I dove over the top headfirst, but he had moved and I landed on my head. They thought I was dead and were trying to come up with a plan to hide my body when I finally came to. Then, one time we were playing tag in an oats field. I was running around looking to tag someone when I saw an opening so I ran and dove head first thinking it was a victim but I was the victim 'cause it was a tree stump. And, then once I was the catcher and my Uncle was batting. Whoever got the ball got to bat, so I cut to his left as he swung and he hit the ball then my forehead. They thought I died on that one too and no one wanted to go to the house to tell what had happened. But, I woke up! I did hit my brother Larry in the head with a hay hook when I was about four. He must have pissed me off. But, that was his head not mine. That is about as far back as I remember. Oh, I did fall on the cross bar of my bicycle while trying to learn to ride when I was five. I hurt my manhood real bad. I've heard people say that has a brain of its own. Does that count as brain damage? If so I need to go back to sports and…"

After all the questions and testing the lady psychiatrist stated the panic attack could have been a result of something called Post Traumatic Stress Disorder, and that the attacks might continue or I might never have another. As of this writing, I've never suffered another panic attack, but I have learned PTSD affects its victims on a subconscious level. I would have numerous problems later in life that I now understand may have been the result of PTSD.

Hope was now working at GTE and we became more and more comfortable with our income. Hope's parents now lived in Kirksville just a 2 ½ hour drive from Grinnell. My parents lived about 30 miles south near Montezuma, Iowa. Dad worked in Grinnell and would stop some Friday nights to pick up the girls for the weekend. Hope and I would pick them up on Sunday. About twice a month in the summer months, we would take off to Baring Country Club in Baring, Missouri. Hope's dad had purchased a cabin on the small 200-acre manmade lake that had been turned into a private country club for people who enjoyed lake activities. He did re-modeling work to the cabin which consisted of one large room with a closed in porch and a bathroom. There was lake water for use in the toilet and sinks but drinking water had to be brought in by containers from Baring, just a ½ mile away. The biggest drawback was a small septic tank with an even smaller French-line. The rule was; toilet paper went into a brown bag for disposal later. No flushing after urination until everyone had gone. Hope's dad found a great deal on a small boat, a Bay liner with an 80 HP motor, and we were set for many years of boating, water skiing, tubing, and the "Green Monster." The Green Monster was a tow tube that sat five people with handles and a runner for your feet on each side. It took a boat awhile to get it up to plane, but once it was gliding on the water, watch out. What fun! The best thing about the Green Monster was trying to stay out of the boats wake and not tip over. The corner and wake could make it tip over and then you had a pile of asses and elbows.

We spent a lot of time teaching the girls to ski as they got older. We also taught friends and relatives children which made the trip to Baring Country Club an enjoyable time for all. A must was the Schlepphorst family reunion for the week of the July 4th Holiday. Hope, her dad, and I would make nightly trips frog hunting on the local area ponds.

He and I would seine for crawfish and run trout lines to catch catfish. Usually on the 4ᵗʰ we would fry up frog legs, boil crawfish, and fry the catfish. All the family would bring potluck dishes to serve and a great meal was had by all. We had people come just to watch us eat the frog legs and crawfish tails but once they got a taste for themselves, they were hooked.

The cabin sits just feet away from the water, and the water depth is a slow gradual change. It's great for younger kids to play in the water and not have to worry about stepping into a hole or drop off. Every morning baths were taken in the lake, shaving by the men was done while standing by the dock waist deep. That is the life!

A little more history about the lake then I'll go on. The lake was manmade by horse teams pulling scrapers to dig out the lake and create a dam and spillway. Hope's grandfather and great grandfather were involved with that work. It was created for the railroad steam engines. The natural slope to the lake from the surrounding area allowed the lake to fill with depths in the middle to probably 20-25 feet. I have a pair of glasses now lying at the bottom of the deepest part of the lake. I wore glasses or contacts to see much of my life but they couldn't be worn while skiing. That was no fun to ski and not see where you are going or enjoy the scenery. So, I thought I could wear my glasses and grab them if I ever started to fall. I was on a slalom ski and cut a sharp turn when the ski went out from under me. I was about four inches from grabbing the glasses as they ripped off my face as I hit the water. Live and learn. Hope and the girls became very good skiers and could get up on the slalom ski. I always had to get up on two then drop a ski. And the card games there have seen a fortune change hands back and forth in the cabin, dimes and quarters at a time. The fun of just enjoying family and friends, food, drinks, and the lazy days of summer was memorable.

After four years in Grinnell, GTE started the process to eliminate the Midwest Company and merge it with another region. My director at the time and I had worked together as peers for about three years. He taught me the process of investigations and security work. He recommended I put in for a new position being created at the World Headquarters for GTE in Stamford, Connecticut for a Security and Safety Manager. I was interviewed, and later offered the job the by the Facilities' Manager. The FM had started years before with GTE when headquarters was in New York City, working in the mailroom. He was a wonderful boss and would later help me during the difficult move process.

Hope and I had a wonderful home in Grinnell, and Mandy had already finished second grade and just started third grade before the move. My commute was a five-minute walk, and we lived close to both parents. With promotion came a tough move to make.

I had taken the job and moved to Connecticut to begin work. What a change for me and the family to face. I went out with a realtor after meeting with a finance person to understand what my salary would allow us to buy. The problem was our home in Grinnell had lost value all four years we lived there. The offer by the buy out company was about what we paid for the old home prior to the work of remodeling and the addition. We had no equity to put down on a new home. GTE did have a second mortgage assistance program that was interest free and no payments required for two years: even with this I knew it was going to be tough to find a home even close to what we were leaving. Three days before Hope came to house hunt I had made a 50 mile range around Stamford and had found nothing but old run down homes that were priced above my maximum loan amount. In addition to all of that, the interest rates were 18% at that time. The night I sat at the airport waiting for Hope to arrive, I cried while sitting in the car. How could I do this to my family just because of a promotion for me? It did not seem right but as life goes on we can look back and see that what we thought was a stupid move turns out to be a smart one. This would be one of those times. Just having Hope with me turned my spirit in a positive direction.

It was a special time for Hope and I, one that took us far from home and the security of being close to our families. Mandy and Buffy were young enough that it would make for an easy transition to a new school. What I was worried about was finding a suitable home in a good school district. As Hope and I looked we were very limited to our price range. We even considered a home that had been converted into a small church in the basement area and did not have a kitchen. It had potential, and it had six bathrooms. It had four heat zones and a blacktop front yard. I told Hope we could cut away the asphalt and leave a great circle driveway. This time Hope could see the possibilities of what could come of this house that needed work in every room. The other plus was it was on a small peninsula called Lordship that had good schools. After days of searching, we were down to making an offer for the church/home or a remodeled saltbox we had found in a Slavic/Catholic neighborhood in Stratford, Connecticut. The home at #5 Winfield Drive was our choice but their asking price was $15,000 above our top mortgage limit. I had spoken with my boss, and with his help I was able to get an additional second mortgage for a down payment that was higher than what my positions was rated for. With that money Hope and I made our top offer at $110,000 thinking the owner would counter with something we could not match.

Hope and I were in for a great surprise. The family had already made on offer on a larger home they needed and were motivated to sell. They accepted our offer as it was. We now had a home we could be happy in, and with wonderful neighbors in a great neighborhood. The girls were excited when they found out the private back yard was equipped with a large above ground pool! We would spend many a night and weekends enjoying the pool and getting the girls to become very good swimmers.

Work was another matter. Not so much the work, the difference was in the five-minute commute in Iowa. If I walked to the train station, it was a 15-minute walk, wait for the train, and then suffer through numerous stops along the 40 miles to Stamford. Then I had another 15-minute walk from the train station to GTE World Headquarters. The people at work were easy to work with, and my boss was great. I was learning new job responsibilities especially on the safety side of the job. Both Security and Safety issues are extremely important but tend to be things employees feel hinders their freedom. With 67 Vice presidents in one building there were many egos to deal with, especially their secretaries who wanted exceptions made to their liking.

Enough of work, what we especially enjoyed was Connecticut and all the happenings available to someone like me. Remember, I had only been to a couple of County fairs, so the culture shock was something I had to grow into. To help with money, Hope got a job with a local Orthopedic Office, and became their best employee within a short period. Hope was not afraid to stand up to one of the doctors who had been notorious concerning his mistreatment of employees. The other employees were afraid of this guy, but the first time he dissed Hope, she went into his office, shut the door and stated, "My father didn't raise me to be a fool and you will not talk to me in that manner." Later, the doctor apologized and from that point forward, he was great with her and even taught her to do things other people didn't do who had worked there for years. I told you before she might be small but she was mighty. But the best thing was she loved me and was my best friend. As long as we were together nothing was going to get the best of us, ever.

Mandy started into the 3rd grade at the local Public School. Buffy was too young to be in kindergarten in Iowa, but she was advanced enough and the school in Stratford decided to let her start even though it was mid year. She could always start over next year if needed, but with her working with Mandy and Hope she never looked back. The girls started at the Catholic school, Holy Name of Jesus, the following school year.

We were far from Iowa and Missouri but Hope's maternal Grandparents lived in Dorchester just outside of Boston. We would make several trips to the Boston area while we were in Connecticut and loved the scenery through Rhode Island and an area of mansions called The Breakers.

Anytime family came to visit, it usually meant a trip to Manhattan with the World Trade Center as a main stop. We also went to our first Broadway show to see "The King and I," with Yule Brenner. Brenner was suffering from cancer and it was close to the end of his performances. He still put on a great show and we really enjoyed the experience. Other side trips included riding the Staten Island Ferry and a visit to the Statute of Liberty. At the time we lived in Connecticut, the statue was being worked on and was covered with scaffolding.

One of our favorite family outings was a brunch at a small motel on the shores of Lordship. There was a nice restaurant with good food and we enjoyed going there after church on Sundays. Each time, we drove pass the church/home and wondered how it turned out.

While we lived in Connecticut, Hope became pregnant with our third child. She seemed to be affected with dramatic mood swings during this pregnancy, but it could have been the stress of dealing with work and home duties. We went as a family to a doctor appointment to check on the baby and listen for a heartbeat. After the excitement of the family hearing the swoosh-swoosh of the babies heartbeat, the doctor scheduled Hope to have an ultrasound. This was a new feature that was starting to be used as standard practice. When Hope went for the ultrasound, they found that the baby had died. The embryo was much too large for Hope's body to absorb on its own. After awhile, a D & C was scheduled, and the baby was taken. After the operation the doctor stated we would not have anymore children because Hope only had half a uterus and had blocked tubes. This was a sad time for us but we had two beautiful healthy girls and felt very fortunate.

In 1986 word started to spread that GTE was going to reduce the work force including some of the corporate staff. Hope and I made a two day drive around this time to the annual Schlepphorst family reunion on the 4th of July. Hope and I drove back nonstop in about 20 hours leaving the girls to spend another two weeks between my parents and hers. When I went into work my boss met with me. He stated that my position had been eliminated, but he was able to convince the decision makers it needed to stay. I had lost my job and regained it in a week's time while on vacation. It prompted me to start checking for other security jobs within the company.

As I checked on jobs, I found out GTE was creating a long distance company to compete with AT&T and MCI. Deregulation was breaking the monopoly of AT&T on long distance and creating new opportunities. GTE Sprint was created, and I heard about a Southeast Regional Security Manager position in Atlanta, Georgia. I called the National Security Manager, who I had met during a Corporate Security meeting in Connecticut the year before. As soon as he knew I was interested, it was a done deal. He hired me on the phone and I was ready to make a trip to Atlanta and begin another house hunt. Only this would be a very exciting and happy time unlike the stress of moving to Connecticut.

What I thought was one of the dumbest moves turned out to be one of the smartest. The housing market from the fall of 1984 to the fall of 1986 had risen dramatically, and when it was all settled we made 78% on the home in Stratford. The only work we had done to the house was painting the bedrooms and hanging wallpaper in the kitchen and bathrooms. We would be able to pay off the second mortgage to GTE and had a nice down payment available for our home in Kennesaw, Georgia. This time when Hope flew in to look at homes I already knew we could simply choose an area with good schools and have almost too many homes to choose from. I had set a price range with a realtor I had been assigned to. She was a nice lady, but a woman that did not understand my dry sense of humor. I was teasing her about showing me homes only in the upper part of the range. I later found out she thought I was serious and upset with her. When Hope and I met with her we had at least three days of looking at nothing but brand new homes in brand new communities with swimming pools and tennis courts. What a change from the last house hunt.

The home we ended up buying was found simply by accident. We were looking at homes in Arden Lake Subdivision and found one that we liked but the yard was steep in the back and we could tell water and mud had gone across the driveway. I told them I wanted to walk the back area so Hope and the realtor drove up and around to meet me at the top of the hill. It was a very hot day 103 degrees and extremely humid. As I came up to the last yard before the cul-de-sac, Hope was inside the house tapping on the window for me to come in. The realtor had told Hope the home was outside our range we had set but Hope wanted to look at it anyway while they were waiting on me. When she went inside she fell in love with its open design and the privacy provided by the cul-de-sac. The realtor was afraid I would be upset. But, I wanted Hope to pick out what she wanted in a home while I was only interested in a nice yard area. This home had both, and we sat with the realtor to offer a lower price to the builder and asked for a refrigerator to be thrown in besides. The realtor told us the builder would never accept our offer but was shocked when during our meeting he looked at the offer and simply said, "OK." As it turned out it was his last home in Arden Lake and he was anxious to go on to other subdivisions. We had our first NEW home at 4251 Edgewater Court, Kennesaw, Georgia. A home we would live in for the next 12 years. I can't say enough for GTE on how they treated us during each move starting with Iowa to Connecticut, then Connecticut to Georgia. They provided full moving assistance with packers, movers, un-packers, and set up. They provided a 3rd party home buying company that eliminated the stress of trying to sell your old home to purchase the next one. They were always fair with the offers.

Our home in Arden Lake was a story and a half design with stucco as the outside finish. The home appeared to be a one story from the front but then became three stories in the back with a full daylight walkout basement, and 1st and 2nd floors. We had 4 bedrooms with a large Master and bath, with an open loft that overlooked to the foyer and living room. It was quite an enormous change from our first home, "the cottage," in Nevada, Iowa. Also, we sat high up with no danger of flooding, and we overlooked the pool and tennis area just a block away. We had no idea at this time how our lives would change during the time spent in this home.

Hope and I became very involved with our church, St. Catherine of Siena, the Catholic Church in Kennesaw. The Catholic group was small at that time in the fall of 1986 but was growing with all the new development going on in the Atlanta area. The church was purchased from the Methodist church that had just moved to their new location.

There was no A/C so any hot days when Mass was held would be outside in the parking lot near a huge oak tree. We became involved in the fund raising drive in 1987 to build a new church on land off Big Shanty Road. The initial construction involved the church and a separate structure for class rooms, offices, and a social hall with a kitchen.

Father Herbert was our priest and someone we fell in love with. He was an Irishman so he could show his emotions from positive to negative when the situation called for it. When the parish started looking for a secretary to help in the office, Hope was their choice. We enjoyed entertaining in our home; and one very special occasion was when a new priest was flying in from Ireland. Our Pastor brought him from the airport directly to our home for his welcoming party. A good time seems to always break out when Catholics start to celebrate. Father Herbert always had a bottle of Johnny Walker Black label set aside at our house for a visit. Our newest priest was a handsome young man with a beautiful singing voice. His entire family in Ireland was well known for their singing talents. Within two years he would fall in love and leave the priesthood to marry. I can't tell you what a loss that was for the church. I have always believed the church must change its canon on Celibacy. So many of its problems, I believe, could be solved with that change alone. But, no one has asked me for my opinion. The Catholic Diocese would suffer an even greater loss when our Bishop was found to be having sexual relations with a beautiful female. The Archbishop was in the honored position for less than two years before he had to step down for having relations with a single mother from the Diocese. The Archbishop was devastated and was "sent away" to be administered back to a celibate life. What a waste of human decency and talent just because the church continues to stand in the past refusing to change. Yet, it has been found guilty of looking the other way and denying its problem with pedophiles in the priesthood.

I was very busy with a work schedule that changed on a daily basis with problems in the telecommunication industry concerning network fraud by computer hackers. Within a year of moving to Atlanta my entire emphasis changed from physical security issues to theft of services on our networks. I say network(s) because the industry as a whole was in transition from an old analog network to new digital networks. As these changes occurred and with the public being naive to new services, the computer hackers and con artists began selling long distance telecom services using stolen services from the main players, AT&T, MCI, and Sprint. By 1988 the Telco companies were loosing millions of dollars in revenue each month. This kept me on the road much of each month but with one plus: frequent flyer miles. Because Delta was the major carrier, I was adding up the miles that would provide many personal travel destinations for the family in the future.

I worked these fraud cases by becoming a customer of the illegal operation. It was easy to do because these people did not want to meet you. The business was handled at a distance, by telephone calls, voice mail boxes, and P.O. Boxes. I would receive tips from people who were introduced to these operations but knew something did not smell right. They would call in and be transferred to me upon which I obtained information about the illegal operation. The informant would introduce me as a friend out of Atlanta via voice mailboxes he was given for messages. I would then become a customer under a fictional name. Payments were sent "cash only" to a P.O. Box. The charge was usually $50 per month for unlimited telephone usage. People would have access via the voice mail or by a direct telephone call with an authorization code for billing purposes. These codes changed almost daily because they would be shut down for fraud. The con artist would tell his customers that the codes were low on minutes and would run out of time. That was one of their scam reasons the codes shut off. It was like buying an expensive watch on a street corner. If you bought it at a low discount, you knew it probably had been stolen.

I had a second line put in my home and the girls knew they weren't allowed to answer it. I am sure they did not understand why. They probably thought I was in the Mafia or something. You know how people can be. They create their own idea about what may be going on without knowing all the facts. I had Hope answer the telephone if I was not at home. Because I traveled so much she had at least the majority of the people talk to her. Two separate people spoke to her and made remarks like "don't speak with an operator if they question you about the code you are using. This is a special promotion they don't know anything about." Right: Hope was instructed just to write down what they said and any codes they gave her. Once I researched the code I could determine who it belonged to and have it cancelled. As our network improved we were able to get the telephone number where the long distance calls were made from. I was working two such operations when we finally got the US Secret Service involved.

Many people are aware of the US Secret Service and their role with executive protection. Most people are not aware they have an investigative unit that works criminal activity such as counterfeit currency and credit card fraud. Because of the amount of fraud in the industry, the Secret Service decided to set up a sting operation to become a customer themselves. They ran their operation out of the Honolulu office and used the name Coconut Connection. I made final written reports on my cases and turned everything over to the Secret Service. By mid year, enough information was obtained on many illegal resellers and search warrants were conducted all over the US including my two cases. Because most of the people arrested were first time offenders, they plead guilty and were ordered to serve probation without any jail time. The defendants in my cases had reasons to fight the charges because they had criminal records and were looking at jail time if they plead guilty. The case went to trial in Honolulu in January of 1989.

For those of you who are not familiar with testimony at trial, I was not able to testify about everything in my investigation. The information provided to Hope by telephone was instrumental in showing the suspects knew they were conducting fraud. In January, Hope and I were both subpoenaed to appear as witnesses for the prosecution. That meant free airfare, free hotel, and $52 each day for meals per person. We flew in on a Wednesday to meet with the US Attorney handling the trial. He met with all witnesses to determine the order of testimony but stated testimony would not begin until the following Tuesday. We were to check in with the US Secret Service each morning by telephone in case something changed or we were needed for anything. Bill and Anna Burbridge, our close friends, had just returned from a Hawaii vacation and had multiple two-day free coupons for rental cars. We rented a car for Thursday and Friday, turned it in, and flew to the Big Island on Friday night using meal money for our round trip airfare from Honolulu to Kona. The Secret Service had made our reservation at the King Kamehameha Hotel for two nights so we were assumed to be federal employees. We paid the Federal rate of $35 per night for a $150 hotel room. We visited Jim and Angela Gannon who had moved to the Big Island after sailing the South Pacific; they had fallen in love with the Hawaiian Islands. Jim was growing about six acres of Kona coffee on his property, and he would sell the beans to the local coffee processing company. Jim and Angela would later buy the Old Hawaii Real Estate Company and raise five children on the island. They still live near Kona at the time of this writing. I will go into detail about Hawaii in a later chapter and combine three more visits by Hope and I with family and friends. Sunday evening we flew back to Honolulu then testified in court Tuesday morning. We flew home Tuesday afternoon filled with wonderful memories and places we would return to the following year. By the way, both defendants were found guilty and sentenced to 10-12 months in prison.

April of 1989 we had enough flyer miles for tickets to vacation during spring break. Bill and Anna Burbridge had become good friends from Arden Lake and their daughter, Sabrina, was right between Mandy and Buffy in age. Bill and Anna had a time-share, and they made reservations for a condo high rise at a beautiful cove south of Acapulco, Mexico called Port of Marquez. Anna, was born in Italy, raised in Paris, and worked at an Air Force base in Germany. Anna was also fluent in Spanish, which made cab rides and restaurant orders no problem. It came in most handy dealing with street vendors. Anna would listen to the vendors talk in Spanish, then in English she would make an offer. Eventually she would know how much they would come down in price. Hope and Anna enjoyed shopping while I enjoyed handing out coins to the young Mexican children walking the streets. It wasn't unusual to see a five year old carrying a baby around with no parent in site.

One night we took a ride in a horse drawn carriage. While the horse was in a full trot we had a young boy jump onto the carriage steps and serenade us with his musical comb and sang "La Bamba." While walking the streets, we came upon a man with his pet monkey outside one of the bars. The monkey was in awe with the glass balls from the ponytail holder in Buffy's hair. He would grab one of the balls then test to see if it was edible then release it with a snap. Another night we went to a carnival far from the strip area. We had to be the only gringo's at the carnival but we were in no danger what so ever. The Mexican people are very kind and caring people. During a market visit Hope joined in with the making of tortillas by a local vendor.

We enjoyed watching the cliff divers, but the day was extremely hot and we had walked up a long hill to get to the viewing area. I don't think the girls were too excited after seeing two or three dives. They probably would have dived in themselves just to cool off.

One of our last days at the resort, we found two young teenagers driving a large ski boat. They were part of a group of skiers who entertained along the shore of Acapulco Bay. They had come south to the Port of Marquez looking for gringo's willing to spend money for skiing and rides. For very little money, the girls received skiing lessons then all of us took a ride north to the Bay of Acapulco. The boys were able to point out the homes of celebrities like Elizabeth Taylor and Sylvester Stallone who had filmed one of his Rambo movies in the area.

Before leaving, Bill and I decided to go on a deep sea fishing trip. The large fishing boat had a crew of three with six passengers, Bill and I, two men from Canada, and a young couple on their honeymoon. The groom was hung over and spent most of his time lying down in the lower bunk area. We left around 8:30am and had been out most of the day with no bites. Sailfish was the main target but none had been seen. Other boat captains kept in touch with each other waiting for news on where the fish were hitting. Late in the afternoon the Captain headed straight out after hearing of some action farther out. I am not sure how far out we were, but the coastline was just a dark outline on the horizon. All of a sudden, sailfish came up all around the bait lines but only one line got a hit. The young newly wed had fought sickness all day, now he had to fight a fish. I had my video camera along and started filming as the sailfish started jumping and fighting the hook. Probably 15-20 minutes later the crew pulled in the fish after knocking it senseless with a club. A beautiful sailfish was the honeymoon prize for the young man. The fish was hoisted up on a scale on the dock, and it turned out to be an 8 foot 120 lb prize. What a great ending to a day of fishing and enjoying the Pacific Ocean.

That summer Hope and I must have had some kind of Anniversary celebration because it wasn't long after I received a call at work. (August 15-16 are my birthday and our anniversary)

"I'm pregnant!"

"Oh Bullshit!"

"I'm telling you, I'm pregnant."

"This isn't April Fools Day Hope."

"I'm pregnant you Goober."

Goober, Asshole, dumb shit, goofy, are a few terms of endearment used by Hope for me.

Hope was pregnant eleven years after she gave birth to Buffy. The doctors obviously don't know what they are talking about sometimes. If God says you are going to have another child, you'll have one. We had already made plans for that Spring break to take the girls to Hawaii. Hope was almost eight months pregnant as we made the trip in April of 1990. Mandy and Buffy were both old enough to appreciate Hawaii, and we decided to spend ten days on the trip: three days on Oahu and the rest of the time on the Big Island. I had enough frequent flyer miles to get all four airfare tickets, and I had ½ price coupons for the Hyatt on Waikiki Beach, oceanfront. When we arrived, the view was gorgeous; the girls were in for a treat. I waited until now to talk about Hawaii and its history because we took Mandy and Buffy to the exact locations Hope and I visited the year before while we waited for the Coconut Connection trial to start. Because of the time change, it is normal for the first two days to be wide-awake about three o'clock in the morning. This is a great time to get an early breakfast and get out on Waikiki Beach and the surrounding areas before the Sun comes up and the streets become crowded with traffic.

I didn't like studying history in high school or college but now I love to read about places in the world and the cultures so much different than our own. There are many great books about Hawaii and its unique history. The people whose lives we changed the most are the Hawaiians themselves once Captain Cook and his men first explored the islands in 1778. I will go into more detail later. Many famous people visited the islands, such as, Robert Louis Stevenson, Mark Twain, and Charles Lindberg. Stevenson was in poor health and the island climates helped him get stronger. He also became friends with one of the last kings, King Kalakaua. Mark Twain wrote a travel book about "The Sandwich Islands," as they were called when he visited. I am jealous to realize most of his exploration was done by horseback. I can only imagine the beauty he found before us "learned people" began our destruction by construction. But Charles Lindberg not only visited the islands, he made his home in an isolated area of Maui, not far from the Sacred Seven Pools near Hanna. He loved the isolation Maui gave him and for someone who had traveled the world, he believed it to be the most beautiful place in the world. He is buried in a small Hawaiian Cemetery not far from where he lived. Prior to his death, he had the small church renovated that stands next to the cemetery.

One of the books I have enjoyed reading is *A Shoal in Time,* by Gavan Daws. It's a great book that discusses how the islands were formed as well as the history of the Hawaiian people. Another amazing story is about Father Damien, a priest from Belgium who spent the last 17 years of his life caring for the Hawaiians who suffered from Leprosy, then died of Leprosy. Both Mandy and Buffy had flown before and were okay with it. Hope had to psych herself and then take Dramamine to dull her senses. The trip from Atlanta was nonstop to Honolulu and took about nine hours. We landed mid afternoon and grabbed a rental car for the ride to Waikiki Beach and the Regency. We spent the rest of the day on the Beach and just walking the shops along Waikiki Beach.

The following day our first stop was Pearl Harbor and a visit to the Arizona Memorial. The tourist center has a lot to see and films to watch, but the real experience is the boat ride to the actual site on the water to the memorial for the men who died on the ship and are entombed in the hull just beneath the water. The next stop is a trip to the North Shore of Oahu to see the famous surfing area called the Banzai pipeline. The trip north took us through the Dole Pineapple Plantation where we enjoyed fresh pineapple and pineapple ice cream. Before we reached the shore we stopped at an old church and a local street side market with all types of home made jewelry, wind chimes, and things made from sea shells. When we finally arrived to the North Shore the waves were spectacular from storms that had taken place far out to sea. This was a red flag day, so no one was allowed to swim or surf because of the dangerous currents. As we continued around the island following the coastline, there were picture perfect moments everywhere: beach areas, tropical vegetation – flowers, and rainbows. We did not have time to stop at the Polynesian Cultural Center located in the small town of Laie, located on the northeast end of Oahu. You need to commit almost an entire day to see the various areas and of course stay for the nightly Luau and dancing. We stopped at Sunset Beach for swimming and body surfing and just to relax and enjoy the beach. Hope got scared when I disappeared while swimming. I had to fight the undertow and rip currents by swimming parallel to the beach until I could swim to shore. I then walked back up the beach to a worried wife. You have to be careful and not fight the currents. On to the Hyatt Regency and shopping and dinner before calling it a long day.

The next day we were off to Diamond Head named by sailors who thought they could see diamonds along the crater top. Most people are familiar with the view of Diamond Head from Waikiki Beach but the best view is the other way around. There is a vehicle tunnel on one side of the crater which is used for vehicle parking and a National Guard Post. After parking the car, you begin a nice leisurely walk along a sidewalk toward the cliff, but then it turns into dirt or mud if it rained recently. On the way to the cliff the trail winds back and forth with steps here and there, then the trail disappears into a tunnel so long it is totally dark inside. The tunnel is very dark, and it is curved, at the end of the tunnel you are looking at a set of stairs almost straight up that are 99 steps high. The girls were running ahead and then would report back as to what we were about to experience. The upcoming adventure was another tunnel with a winding staircase to the next level, a WWII gun concrete bunker. Hope thought this part was easy because she didn't have to stoop down for the low ceiling. But, at 6'3" I found it uncomfortable. Then, out of the bunker and more climbing of the outside trail to the top. The view is exceptional of the Waikiki Beach and the High Rise Hotels. The city can be seen in its entirety and another crater off in the distance, Koko Head. We spent quite a bit of time enjoying the view, the rest, and the peace one feels from just being in Hawaii. Many of the mansions can be seen far down below with their beautiful ocean views, the tennis courts and swimming pools. One can dream of someday owning one of them. At the end of the trip down, two oriental men saw Hope was heavy in pregnancy, "You go clear to top?" and after Hope responded yes, they commented, "You have Astronaut Baby!"

The next stop was Hanauma Bay, just east of Honolulu. The Bay was made famous by Elvis Presley's movie, *Blue Hawaii,* in which he played a beach bum/singer living on the beach. His beach home was a movie set on Hanauma Bay. The bay is actually a low volcanic crater that the ocean cut through on one part of the crater. The ocean swept over the crater floor creating a natural area for coral to grow and fish to make their homes. The inside arch makes up most of the beautiful beach. The girls and I loved floating around looking at the beautiful colors of the fish. I could only get Hope to wade and drop green peas for the fish to come to the surface to eat. While she enjoyed this, she would realize on another trip how enjoyable snorkeling could be. The end of this day was a stop at a nice restaurant and included sidewalk shopping.

The last day on Oahu was started by what we thought would be a leisurely hike to Manoa Falls just outside of Honolulu. It had rained the evening before, and the sidewalk trail soon turned to mud. The mud trails soon turned to slippery rocks and fallen logs, which made it even hard to determine where the trail was. Hope was scared but determined to make it to the falls. We were all very nervous when the trail wrapped around a cliff with a straight drop off and a very narrow foot path. Once we made Manoa Falls we were mud up to our waists. Hope sat in the shallow cold water at the base of the falls while Mandy, Buffy, and I swam and played on the slippery rocks. Hope was worried enough for two people, rightfully so. It was almost a private waterfall with only a local college student reading/studying while we were there. We made a slow muddy walk back to the car and were so happy to get there without anyone falling, especially Hope. It was years later I remember hearing or reading about some people being killed at the falls when a rockslide occurred. Nature can be so beautiful but dangerous at the same time. Back to Honolulu; turn in the rental car then on to Kona and the "Big Island."

The Kona airport sits on the edge of the Pacific Ocean on an old lava flow. The entire airport is outdoors with thatch-roofed buildings for restrooms or baggage claim. A short bus ride had us at the rental car and off to Kona just a few miles south of the airport. We checked in again at the King Kamehameha Hotel and had time to make a visit with Jim and Angela and their children. Jim had completed a second floor master bedroom with a beautiful view of the Kona Coastline at about 1,000 feet above sea level. Before our visit the previous year, I had never eaten grilled tuna. When Jim said he was grilling tuna I wondered how you could do that with tuna out of a can. Grilled tuna, fresh from the market, is as good as a filet Mignon from the best restaurant you know.

The next day we took off from Kona at sunrise heading south along the coast toward our first destination, the painted church. This church was one of many that Father Damien built prior to his move to the Leprosy Colony on Molokai. The church is totally painted inside with beautiful religious scenes and has beautiful garden areas around the outside and cemetery area. Next stop is the Volcano National Park at the southeast side of the island.

The drive to the active volcano of Kilauea changes scenery multiple times from beautiful coastal views, to coffee plantations, to Macadamia Nut Trees, to open pasture areas, to scraggly bush areas, and to nothing grows areas. The black lava fields look from the car as rich farmland but it is a solid lava desert where almost nothing grows. As you work your way around to the park, you begin to rise in elevation and pass by residential areas where the roads are cut through the lava. The areas where the homes are built are rich with flora but nothing grows in the five-acre lots that stand empty. Rain is still scarce in this part of the island and residents use the "catchment system" to capture the rain as it runs down roofs into a large holding tank near each home. The volcanic soil is rich with nutrients but needs mans help to provide the needed moisture. As we near the park entrance there is more tree and shrub growth seen along the highway. But, it becomes easy to spot recent lava flows where the vegetation simply disappears. The first stop is the visitor center overlooking the main crater of Kilauea. Steam rises from cracks in the crater floor but this is not where the main lava flows to the ocean. The steam smells like rotten eggs. Videos inside the center show the various levels of activity over the years and earthquake instruments show the constant tremors occurring all around the mountain. The elevation is 1,222 meters or 4009 feet here, so the temperatures are usually 10-20 degrees cooler than at the beach, which can be around 40-50 degrees in the winter months. The drive is beautiful from the visitors' center to the ocean where other areas such as steam vents, lava tubes, and other in-active craters can be explored. You'll know where to park near where the lava enters the ocean because you'll see the huge clouds of steam and the road ends where the last lava flow crossed it. At the times we have been to this area, the road has been crossed many times by a new lava flow. The walk to the area where lava flows into the ocean is an easy walk, but a walk where you must watch your step. Ropes are usually set up to warn people not to go closer. But, people have been known to ignore the warnings and push their luck. It is amazing to stand on part of the island that was created in just a short span of time.

Our next stop is Hilo where we grab lunch and enjoy the atmosphere on the rainy side of the island. During the drive from the volcano area to Hilo means driving through rain at some point. But, then the sun breaks through and amazing rainbows can be seen, sometimes double rainbows. If there is gold at the end of rainbows then most of the gold is on the Big Island. If I hadn't mentioned it before, the island is named Hawaii the same as the state. But, it is usually referred to as the Big Island because it is larger than all the other islands combined. It has two mountains, Mauna Kea to the north and Mauna Loa to the south. Both mountains are over 13,000 feet above sea level and if measured from their base on the ocean floor they are both higher than Mt. Everest. Snowcaps can be seen on both mountains at certain times of the year. The Big Island is also unique in the fact that most of the climates of the world exist on this one island.

After lunch, we are off going North of Hilo to a small rainforest area that is home to Akaka Falls. We made a stop in a small town on the highway to get ice cream, then a few miles drive through sugar cane fields and you have arrived in the parking lot. The walk is relatively easy for a pregnant woman compared to Diamond Head and Manoa Falls. Akaka Falls is 440 feet high and if it has been raining over a few days, you will hear the roar of the falls long before you see them. When the water flow is heavy, you are unable to see the bottom because of the water vapor rising up through the valley below. The observation point is across the valley and just below the top of the falls. This is a great photo opportunity with not only the falls, but the trees, shrubs, and flowers seen along the walk. Someday I would like to take one of the helicopter rides from Hilo to see the area from the sky.

There are many stops along the way to visit Macadamia tree farms and processing plants. These nuts are delicious white balls and are good alone, chocolate covered, or in brittle. The groves of trees are well-manicured rows, and they thrive in the rainy areas of the island.

Our next stop is the Parker Ranch on the North side of the island.

The ranch is approximately 250,000 acres and currently owned by the workers who took over ownership after Richard Smart passed away in 1992. Generations have worked on the ranch that was first started by John Palmer Parker (1790-1868) who jumped ship around 1809 and ended up marrying Kipikane (1800-1860) who was part of the Royal Family. The Hawaiian cowboys are called Paniolo and can be seen rounding up cattle all over the ranch. This amazing area is one of the largest ranches in the US with grass pastures, cactus patches, and herds of cattle and horses with a backdrop of Mauna Kea in the distance. Areas of the ranch are watered by large pipelines built to carry water from areas with 300 plus inches of rain each year to areas with 10 inches or less. The Waimea community is an area that has developed because of the ranch and contains a Parker Ranch museum. After leaving Parker Ranch, it is a choice to drop down along the coast and back to Kona or cross the open areas at the base of Mauna Kea with its open grass ranges with beautiful views all the way to Kona. We arrived back to Kona as the sun sets on our long but wondrous day of adventure. Off to a great restaurant, this could be any of the many along the Kona Coastal Street, before heading back to the hotel.

The King Kamehameha Hotel is a museum of the Hawaiian culture with large pictures of all the royalty from Kamehameha to the last royal Princess Victoria Ka`iulani. The Kona coast is known for its deep-sea fishing with replicas of Marlin world records hanging on the walls of the hotel. Replicas of a Hawaiian home stand outside the hotel along the large oceanfront. This harbor is famous for the opening 2.4 mile swim for the Iron Man competition held each year.

The next few days go quickly while visiting with Jim & Angela and family, snorkeling at a local park area and just relaxing at one of the many beaches along the Kona Coast. The last day we ate brunch at a local resort then made trips back to the airport.

37

Sarah

Hope stood the test while pregnant and enjoyed showing Mandy and Buffy Hawaii. A baby girl had flown to Hawaii, climbed Diamond Head, and walked along Waikiki. Sarah Michelle Hope Thomas was born on May 25, 1990, at Northside Hospital in Atlanta. The birthing rooms are large and Mandy and Buffy were allowed into the room during Sarah's birth. She was a large baby and things turned hectic when the monitors showed she was in distress then her heart stopped. With Hope pushing with everything she had, the doctor pulled Sarah out with no vital signs; the cord had been wrapped around her neck. With quick action by the doctor and nurses, they got Sarah's throat clear, and we all were elated when she started to cry. I am sure Mandy and Buffy were scared by the last few minutes but quickly responded to see Sarah get cleaned up then handed around the room to the girls and finally to Hope. Another beautiful girl who weighed in at almost ten pounds joined the Thomas family.

By that fall Sarah was being passed around in the stands during football games. Mandy was on the cheerleading squad and Buffy was their mascot cheerleader. We took Sarah to every game and tried to pass her off but she would always get passed back to us by the end of the game. We decided to keep her.

The doctor's had told us we would never have children again yet

Sarah came eleven years after Buffy. Because she would be raised like an only child, we wanted to have another child to give her a playmate. We had always talked about having four children, but it took eleven years for Sarah to come what were the odds.

38

Jackie

Well, 16 months later we found ourselves at Northside Hospital again, here came our fourth daughter Jacqueline Mickaela Schlepphorst Thomas. Jackie, named after her Grandfather, was born on September 20, 1991 and was bigger than Sarah, Jackie was ten pounds. Mandy and Buffy declined to be in the room after the other ordeal with Sarah. Jackie was the same issue getting hung up on the way out and her vital signs disappeared. The Doctor had her by the head and pulled her the rest of the way. We didn't know until the following day that she had both collarbones broken and pulled muscles on one side of her neck. She would have to have many hours of therapy on her neck given at home by Hope. Hope had done therapy for Buffy who had a foot misshaped because of how she was carried in the womb. It was discovered that Jackie had Torticollis, also caused by a position deformity, how she was carried in the womb. This was due to her large size. Hope went above and beyond and fixed both children's issues until there was no way to tell either had a problem.

It was time for me to declare the end of our child bearing days. I made it so any further children would require DNA testing. We had our four girls, and that was enough plus Sarah had her playmate. From this point on we were raising two sets of children. Two separate times we went to parent orientation for a college student one night and parent orientation for pre-school the next. Hope had quit the secretary position with the Parish to be home with Sarah and then Jackie so they both matured rapidly. They had Mandy and Buffy, and other older kids around much of the time so they advanced quickly.

39

Maui

By 1995, it was time to make another trip to Hawaii. Bill and Anna went also and had a condo available on Maui through their time-share. Hope and I had not been to Maui yet, so we looked forward to seeing new sites of paradise. Mom and dad were still living in Monet, Missouri and I had enough frequent flyer miles for two more tickets. Mom and dad would fly into Maui toward the end of the first week and then all of us went on to Kona and the Big Island for our second week.

Maui is a beautiful island made up of two islands connected by a low flat plain. West Maui has Lahaina and the Kaanapali area, while east Maui has the county seat Wailuku and Hanna on the far side, and Kihei on the Southern coast. Bill and Anna had a condo available in Kihei for our base of operation. When you stay in paradise the room is for sleeping only, the rest of the time is for exploration of the island.

Maui is much smaller than the Big Island but is much more developed. This creates more traffic so a round trip tour of the island takes an entire day as well. Lahaina is an old whaling port with great restaurants and shops. Near the marina stands one Banyan tree that covers an entire city block. I am a fan of old trees so that is one reason I love Hawaii with its Banyan, Monkey Pod, Eucalyptus, Kukui, Plumeria, and the many other common trees found there. They grow to huge dimensions in a climate that allows growth year round.

From the Marina we jumped on a tour boat that took us across the ocean channel to the island of Lanai for a snorkeling trip. After snorkeling along the beach, we went ashore for lunch and a wagon ride along a road leading to an old sugar plantation. Then back on the boat and the trip back to Maui. We saw some whales far away, but not many were left during that time of the year.

From Lahaina we headed around the North side past Napili Point and on to the blowhole. The blowhole shoots a spray of water each time a large wave comes in and is readily accessible and safe to get close enough for a great photo opportunity. This area of Maui is very remote with high cliffs overhanging to the ocean and the main road turns into a dirt road. We had passed an area where we saw surfers, so we made a stop there to watch. Surfers have to have a strong sense of their ability because the waves can take them into dangerous areas of volcanic rock at or just under the water levels.

It was time to head for Kihei to enjoy the rest of the evening on the condo beach area and prepare for dinner. Our next day stop would start early because we were headed for the summit of Haleakala, a ten thousand foot volcano with a crater large enough to fit the island of Manhattan inside. The point of the adventure was to be there to watch the sunrise over the crater walls. The next morning we headed up the mountain road and reached the top well before sunrise. At ten thousand feet and without the sun it is a challenge to stay warm. Most people going to Hawaii on vacation don't pack for cold weather, so take along a blanket or two from their hotel room. The site is well worth the effort of getting up early and putting up with the cold. Once the sun is up there are trails to walk and even over night cabins in the crater for the hiking enthusiasts. There are plants and animals to be seen such as the Silver Sword plant and the Nene goose that are found no other place in the world. And the peaceful quietness at this height is a pleasure to enjoy before heading back down. For bicycle riders, you can pay for a tour that takes you to the top to see the sunrise then you ride a bicycle down the well-paved road to the bottom. The views are spectacular but don't forget to watch the road.

The next day we were off on the "Road to Hana." The road to Hana is a two-lane road but has many one-lane bridges. Depending on the time of your visit and the amount of traffic will determine how long it will take. I would recommend taking your time and stop at the many waterfalls along the way. Hana is pricey because of its seclusion so expect to pay more for lunch unless you bring it with you. Past Hana is the Seven Sacred Pools. It is said these pools were only for royalty and any common person caught swimming there would meet their maker. While at the Seven Pools I asked the local ranger how to find Charles Lindberg's gravesite. I had read a biography of him and knew he was returned to this area once he knew he was dying of cancer and was buried in a small Hawaiian cemetery. Lindberg in all his travels of the world stated these islands were the most beautiful place in the world. The problem in 1995 was the paved road stopped just past the park and the rest of the trip was on a dirt/rock road. The park ranger said the only way to identify the turn off was by looking for a red barn on the right side. The first lane to the left past the barn would go back into a field then into a canopy of trees. It dead-ended at the church and cemetery. We enjoyed visiting the plain marker under a large tree. It might seem like a lonely place for such a great man but one is able to look at the ocean below and understand how he felt about this area. The church had been renovated with Lindberg's funding and some floor repair was being done at the time of our visit. Hope enjoyed speaking with the woman fixing the grass woven floor.

As we returned to the road and continued west we came upon a winery and small store. We were able to taste the local wine, and it is always interesting to speak with the friendly locals. We headed to Kihei, and to another great day of adventure.

The next morning I tried talking someone into going on a helicopter ride but no one volunteered. Bill took me to the airport where I boarded a Hawaiian Blue copter that would rise to the top of Haleakala and speed across the crater floor toward the opening on the opposite side where the last lava flow poured over the crater edge. At high speed we went from being about 100 feet off the ground, and then the bottom dropped out from under us as we came across the mountains drop off to the ocean. The chopper dropped to the ocean and then followed the islands edge until we came to a waterfall. The chopper rose slowly to the top of the waterfall then zipped up the river below tree top high. Eucalyptus trees lined both sides of the river as we continued on the river's path up to another waterfall. The chopper hovered at the base turning to both sides for the photo opportunity, and then slowly rose to the top and up the river again. We swung over toward Hana and over property owned by George Harrison of the Beatles and Jim Nabors who sang and played Gomer Pyle. Only the baby boomers will remember him. On to the airport and the ride was over, almost one hour of excitement and well worth the cost.

That weekend my parents flew into Maui and they stayed in a local hotel for two nights. They had never traveled so far and they were excited about the chance to see Hawaii. The next day they would see more than they had planned. We took a short drive to Mahina Beach, a beautiful beach with relatively no one on it. But there were many cars in the parking lot, more cars than people. We noticed some of the folks going over a ridge at the end of the beach, so everyone but me decided to follow and check out the other side. What they found was a nude beach. Another photo opportunity, I guess Dad was so focused he didn't see a large wave and almost got knocked down. Bill and Anna were used to the nude beaches in Europe and all I understood Hope to say was, "Why isn't Mick that big!?" I knew it wasn't a good idea to let her go. The next day before our flight to Kona and the Big Island, we visited Iao Valley Needle State Park. The needles were the cooled lava tubes of old volcanoes where the crater had been washed away over eons leaving only the lava standing against the elements. A fast running river worked its way through the park with many small falls along the way. One of the formations of the natural lava rock is a remarkable likeness of the profile of John F. Kennedy. It is about fifty feet high and visible from the road.

We went to the airport, and headed off to Kona. Hope and I had made arrangements to rent a condo across the highway from a beautiful little beach area. We gave up the master to mom and dad and slept on the balcony on a mattress where we could enjoy the sounds of the waves and the interior garden of the complex. Jim and Angela joined us one night for a cook out and we enjoyed their stories of sailing to Hawaii and the South Pacific. Our tour took us to the regular sites, Volcano National Park, Mauna Kea Macadamia Nut Plantation, Hilo, Akaka Falls, Parker Ranch, and back to Kona. On this trip, we made a stop south of Kona to the Kona Coffee Plant. Outside the plant were mature Plumeria trees that were in bloom. The Plumeria bloom is used in making the greeting leis, and the aroma is wonderful. We enjoyed watching the coffee bean process all the way to ground coffee. Of course, we had to buy the original to bring home.

It is always sad on the last day because two weeks is not enough time when visiting the islands. Anything less than two weeks is a shame. I am sure the folks enjoyed their vacation but mom and I had planned to take a helicopter ride from the Volcano National Park. Our visit to the park had been delayed by four days when the park was closed because of a death. A photographer had gotten too close to the lava flow and the shelf he was on collapsed into the ocean water, which is boiling. His body was never recovered. The day we were able to visit was a cloudy, rainy day, and not a day to ride a chopper. As we all sat at the Kona airport waiting for our flight each of us reflected on this vacation; memories we would file away for a lifetime.

40

Grandparents

That same year, the day Sarah turned five, Hope, and I became grandparents; Austin Reece Thomas Grant was born on May 25, 1995. Their second son, Corey Taylor Grant was born on March 21, 1997, and our only granddaughter to date, Erika Heather Grant was born on 9/11/1999. They are great kids with normal kid problems now and then. As parents, Chris and Mandy stress over each issue, as grandparents, Hope and I offer support but smile in our hearts knowing it will pass. Chris and Mandy have made a beautiful life together as they celebrate their 20th year of marriage.

41

Off to Hawaii

Before I go on to our last trip to Hawaii with Kenny and Jodi Hewatt, I have to tell a funny story about our trash and a great big black bear. It must have been right after Easter of 1994. Mandy had been out and returned home right around midnight, so Hope and I were still awake. Within a few minutes, we heard a noise from the trashcan and Hope got up to look out the window. I felt it must be a raccoon trying to get the lid off and when Hope announced, "It's a Bear!" I said, "Bullshit, it can't be a bear!" but she replied with an astounding, "I'm telling you it's a BEAR!" So I went down stairs to prove her wrong, but when I turned on the lights for our deck; "It's a bear!" The black bear was lying at the bottom of the steps eating something from the trash. I believed it must be injured and was going anywhere to get food.

We called the police right away; I had dealt with a bat on my own for a while but I wasn't going to deal with a bear. When the police car pulled into the drive the bear stood up on its hind legs to look around. This was a big bear, not just a young one. The bear had moved away from the step area as the officer came to the front door. You could tell he thought we were on drugs or something. He stepped out on the deck with me right behind him. As he turned his flashlight on to look over the edge of the deck, the bear stood up again and was face to face with us. The officer stepped all over me as he retreated to the house calling on his radio, "It is a BEAR! CONFIRM! It is a BEAR! BEAR is in the backyard!" We heard the bear run off through our back woods, and the Georgia DNR seemed uninterested in finding the bear. The next morning I got a call from Hope. "There are TV trucks out here in the cul-de-sac and reporters want to get a story about the bear." We had determined the bear had smelled out Easter candy thrown away in the trash after it melted in a bag in the back of the van. That night I saw a view of our back yard and the trash can as a cameraman walked through the woods at bear level. And, of course Hope told all of Atlanta I didn't believe it was a bear. Within two weeks, a large black bear was killed when hit by a car as it crossed Wooten Lake Road, about a 1/2 mile from our home.

Off to Hawaii, our last trip but hopefully not our final trip. This trip again was with Kenny and Jodi who had not been there before so we planned a three-day stay in Oahu, then four days in Kona, and the last three days in Maui. We would prefer to stay longer but Jodi had not been away from her family for any length of time before and we were lucky to get the ten days. We wanted them to see Honolulu and the "must" see things but also wanted them to get a feel of the other islands. The main difference during this trip was our stay on Maui at Napili Point. Kenny & I swam with sea turtles face to face in the bay just below our condo. Our trip to Haleakala was to watch the sunset instead of the sunrise. At this height, you can see the Big Island, Lanai, and Molokai as the sunsets over Lanai.

42

Leper Colony; Kalaupapa

The next trip was for me alone. Even though I offered the others to join me, I was expecting them to decline. If you had a choice to lie on a beach or visit a leper colony; well, they chose the beach but dropped me off at the West Maui Airport. I had read *Holy Man: Father Damien of Molokai,* by Gavin Daws, a professor at the University of Hawaii. I always wanted to visit the colony but had not set the time aside to make the trip. Knowing not when I would get back, I decided this was the time to go. I caught a small prop plane that held about 10-15 passengers when full. There was me and one other person aboard as we took off from Maui and flew across the channel to Molokai and on along the North shore. This is one of the most beautiful and most remote areas of all the islands. The ocean has eaten away at the island creating two thousand foot cliffs all along its north shore with water falls here and there dropping to the ocean. We flew over the cliffs and landed at the one and only airport. The one passenger got off and three others boarded for our flight back to Kalaupapa, a ten square mile peninsula jutting off the bottom of the cliffs almost in the center of the island. The landing strip at the far Northern point started just after the ocean and ended just before the ocean. Coming in to land seemed like a very precise plan with little room for error; short you land in the ocean, long you end up in the ocean. Fortunately, the guy had done it before and we had a safe landing. As we got off the plane, the pilot handed us a sack lunch and a bottle of water. He stated he would be back in about 4-5 hours to pick us up. He stated the tour bus would be there to pick us up shortly. The facilities at this airport amounted to restrooms and an open sitting area with a roof. No one manned a post because there was nothing to be done. After waiting for about 20 minutes, we heard a vehicle approach over the bumpy, rocky, and dusty road.

I am sure the others, like me, expected the tour bus to be something like what you ride to a rental car lot; air conditioned with nice comfy seats. Not so; as the old school bus approached it was hard to tell it was yellow from all the rust. The air conditioning was on 'cause all the windows were open. Out of the bus came what most would refer to as "a grumpy old man," with disheveled hair and clothes. He had a list of guests and started calling off our names as if we were reporting to boot camp. He made a comment about someone not showing up to drive so he was our guide for the day.

Everyone got on board and I slide into the first seat behind him so I could hear what was said, seeing there was no PA system. The driver said nothing as we bounced along the pot hole filled road then stopped just outside the village at a cemetery. He commented that those still living here at the colony are now buried in this cemetery. He stated, "My brother is the most recent grave." It is at that time we realize he is not only our driver and guide but he is living in the colony. He goes on to introduce himself as Richard Marks. He came to Kalaupapa when he was 15 years old after being diagnosed with leprosy. He said it appeared shortly after he was injured in a motorcycle accident, and he and most of his family lived here at one time. Richard was one of the youngest still living in the colony, and I believe he said there were about 50 people still living there. Most of them never left the village even though they were cured of leprosy. "Hansen's Disease" it is now called after the man who discovered sulfone drugs that stopped the damage of the human tissues and organs. Richard stated his leprosy was stopped before any damage was done but not so for many still living there. He said we could not film or take pictures in the village. We were to respect the privacy of those who lived there, but Richard was fine for anyone who wanted to film him or take pictures.

Our next stop was the base of the cliff where the only trail is ended at a corral with mules. Many of the folks going on the tour have the option of riding down the cliff trail on mules. One young couple chose to hike down. Richard went through his list again and everyone took their seat. After the mule ride, I'm sure they enjoyed the comfort of the bus seats. Once in the village, we stopped at the Catholic Church, St. Francis. The cemetery is where Mother Marianne is buried. Mother Marianne Cope was a young nun from Syracuse, NY who heard of Father Damien and his need for help in the leprosy colony. She and other nuns from the Sisters of the Third Order of Saint Francis in Syracuse petitioned the Hawaiian Government for over four years before finally being allowed to go to Kalaupapa. It was just in time to care for Father Damien as he lay on his deathbed, a victim of leprosy, after seventeen years of caring for the people of the colony. The nuns, mostly in their early 20's spent the remainder of their lives caring for the leprosy victims. The nuns lived away from the colony on the western side of the peninsula in the village that exists today. The Eastern side, known as Kalawao is where Father Damien lived among the victims. He was a carpenter Priest and used his building skills to build churches on both Maui and the Big Island before going to Molokai. He built a church on the main portion of Molokai and made the walk many times up the cliff trail for meetings and a chance to take communion and give confession. Later, once he became ill with leprosy, he was denied permission to leave the colony. During his seventeen years at the service of the leprosy sufferers, he would work cleaning wounds and changing bandages, then work long hours building a church and living compounds for the colony. His story is full of frustration because of the politics, both from the church and the Hawaiian Government, in obtaining the supplies he needed through those years.

We stopped at a local bookstore where I purchased *Pilgrimage & Exile: Mother Marianne of Molokai*. This book continues the story of the colony after Father Damien is laid to rest. Joseph Dutton was a lay person who had joined Father Damien years earlier. Dutton continued to work with Mother Marianne and other nuns who volunteered to spend their lives helping the people suffering from leprosy. Before leaving, we stopped at Richard Marks' home so he could eat something. We waited in the bus.

The rest of the tour we traveled to the Eastern section of the peninsula to Kalawao. Here stands the church St. Philomena that Father Damien built in 1873. He died in 1889, yet his grave no longer holds his body because it was moved to Tremolo, Belgium in 1936. His right hand was returned to this gravesite in 1995 at the request of the colony residents. Richard Marks talked the entire tour of the history of the colony and the troubles faced by Father Damien. He also spoke about a movie to be made that would be released sometime in 1999. He believed Robin Williams was being persuaded to play Father Damien. Richard would be involved along with others in the colony to provide input and to be stand-ins when needed. The movie was released in 1999 but Robin Williams did not play a part. I recommend it to all along with any number of books now published about Kalaupapa and Father Damien.

We stopped at a beautiful opening overlooking the bay where years before the lepers were thrown off ships no matter whether they could swim. Anything they were allowed to bring was thrown in after them. The healthy males on shore would fight over any woman and belongings they wanted for themselves. That peaceful day with its beauty made it hard to imagine those acts occurred just below where we sat and ate our sack lunch.

We evidently had spent too much time in the area because Richard was driving hard to get us back to the other side and on to the mules. The road was rough, and the bus bounced all over the road. I am sure those in back were getting a ride they didn't expect. Once at the mule corral, those who were riding or walking back got off and away we went to the airport. Once there, myself and two other men shook Richard's hand and thanked him for all he had shown and told us. Richard seemed emotional about the fact that we were not afraid to shake his hand. The plane arrived, and we were off to the Molokai airport and then took off for West Maui. It was an experience beyond anything I have seen in Hawaii and I hope to return to visit Richard's grave. He passed away December 9, 2008. As I came off the plane to meet Hope, Kenny, and Jodi, I am sure they could see that I had been moved from the experience.

43

Country Club of Mount Dora

We had many happy times in Kennesaw but a job opening within Sprint was available in the local division in Leesburg, Florida and I decided to make the move. With Mandy married and Buffy in college at Georgia State, I felt Florida would be a good move for us and the younger girls. With Orlando not far away, we knew family and friends would make the trek south and keep us full with visitors. I felt the change would keep me at home more and I would not miss the young girls grow up. In Georgia, I traveled constantly and was not happy with my situation there.

My office was in Leesburg and I would cover most of Central Florida from Starkville to Okeechobee. But, I would be home each night if I needed to be. We found a new home in the Country Club of Mount Dora just half way between my Leesburg office and the state headquarters in Apopka. Once we decided on living in a golf community I insisted Hope learn to play golf. Both her parents are golfers and I wanted to spend as much time with her when not working. In a golf community, it was easy to find husband and wives we could golf with and make new friends.

The club had tennis courts and a wonderful pool for Sarah and Jackie to enjoy. But their main fun was the trips to New Smyrna Beach and playing in the waves and sand. It was only a one and a half hour drive to New Smyrna with a McDonald's strategically placed on the way in. We would stop there for lunch, spend 2-3 hours on the beach and we could be back for a round of golf before dark.

We spent Christmas of 1998 in Florida. After opening gifts in the morning we headed out for New Smyrna, ate lunch, then spent the afternoon on the beach. Jackie, who was seven at the time, said, "Dad, Florida's just a wonderful place to live." We all agreed with her. Each morning as I went to work I would be jealous because my neighbors would be on the second tee box. When I came home, Hope and I could jump on the golf cart (everyone had a golf cart door and space in the garage) and drive onto the course anywhere we wanted to start playing. It was like having a private course at early evening.

A great part of living in Central Florida was the Orange Trees. An Orange Grove and an open pasture with cattle bordered our back yard. There is nothing like the smell of Orange Blossoms coming in your window of the house or in your car as you drive the countryside. One morning I noticed a new born calf lying near our fence line, and it had not even got up yet to suck.

As Hope and I sat on the Lanai one Saturday morning, we heard a huge explosion. The cows in the field were even startled by the sound and were staring off in the distance. I heard later that it was the sonic boom from a returning space shuttle. I vowed to watch the next shuttle take off. I was in my Leesburg office one day and heard a shuttle was to take off about 1:00pm. I had just enough time to get there, so I called my boss and took the afternoon off. As I got close to Merritt Island, the traffic was parked on both sides of the road and I had no idea where to go to get a good view. I turned North on the road and went a few miles before coming to a church parking lot. A school bus had just parked and kids were getting of. The launch had been delayed a few minutes, so I had time to get into the parking spot as the count down started. There was a large opening toward the East with a tree line at the end. As lift off occurred we had no idea where to look for it. Then, it rose up in the opening coming over the tree line. I could not have had a better view. The cool part was seeing the shuttle first then all of a sudden; the air was crackling from the roar of the rocket engines. You can actually feel the sound waves against your face. What a site it was, one I'll never forget.

After talking with Hope we made a plan to determine when the next night launch would be and take Sarah and Jackie to watch. A few months later, we were on our way to a launch. It seems like it was delayed later than planned, but we let the kids sleep as we drove. Again, I was not sure where to stop and we ended up quite a ways away. But, it did not matter because the rocket lit the entire sky as if the sun was coming up. It was quite a site, to see and hear.

44

Sprint World Headquarters

I had a decision to make after being in Florida just 15 months. After the company reorganized, I was moved into physical security. My decision was to stay in Florida and take a two level demotion, or move to Kansas City, Sprint World Headquarters for a two level promotion. There really was no choice; besides, Hope's parents lived in Kirksville, Missouri and she had many relatives in the KC area. Looking back now, staying in Florida would have been the best thing for us but I can't dwell on that any further.

We found a nice home in Overland Park near where Sprint is head-quartered. It was a home with a flat drive but dropped off very steeply in the backyard. We backed up to a par 3 hole on the Iron Horse Golf Course. It turned out to be a great place for us to sled in the winter-time. Sarah and Jackie may have seen snow but had no experience with it like they would find in Kansas. My travel away from home was less than in Georgia and it was planned travel, which helped on being home for family time.

The girls were close to good schools and Hope continued working in the school system as a paraprofessional for special education stu-dents. She had started this work when we were in Florida and would continue in each school system we went to.

The great thing about Kansas was we were close enough to Baring,

Missouri to spend more time with Hope's folks at the cabin. The girls totally enjoyed the lake and would spend the entire day in the water. Hope's dad and I didn't spend as much time running trout lines but we still hunter for frogs if it was a good season. Her dad had noticed that blue herons were coming father north in the summer and could wipe out a pond from frogs in short order. Farmers had found dead blue herons that had as many as ten frogs in their stomach. If you've never been to northeast Missouri you owe it to yourself to visit and enjoy the countryside views and the people. I call it Mark Twain territory because it is only about 40 miles or so to Hannibal.

While living in KC, I covered the Western Region starting at Denver up to Seattle to Honolulu and down to San Diego, Phoenix, and Albuquerque, NM. During my career with Sprint, I was able to travel to most of the states and enjoy seeing most of the country.

On 9/11/1999, our third grandchild with Mandy and Chris was born, a little girl, Erika Heather Grant. Hope had planned to be there for the delivery, but Erika decided to come a few days early. Hope only missed the delivery by a few hours. Erika was born healthy, but within a matter of six months, something was terribly wrong; she started to bleed internally. She was having as many as 10-12 diapers a day with blood soaking the diaper. She was placed in Scottish Rite Children's Hospital in Atlanta with the doctors unsure of what her problem was. As more and more tests were conducted many of the doctors could not believe what the test were showing, ulcerative colitis. The reason they could not agree was the fact there were no medical records ever showing the disease at such an early age. U.C. mostly affects young adults in their 20's to 30's, not a young baby.

The treatment was also a concern with the doctors because steroids and immune inhibitors had to be administered to stop the bleeding. The concern was, what amounts should be given. A young child with her immune system stopped could allow any sickness to be lethal. The other problem was how to use enough steroids to stop the bleeding without harming her normal development. Erika went from a 95% rating in height and weight shortly after birth to as low as a 5% rate toward the end of treatment. It was doubly hard to see a grandchild hurting and crying in the hospital and your daughter is also hurting and crying. Once Sarah and Jackie were out of school in May of 2000, Hope and the girls went to Georgia to help Mandy. She had two young boys at home while Chris was working and a baby in and out of the hospital over a 40-day period. Sarah and Jackie were young girls, but they had to be relied on to help take care of the boys and do chores around the house. With thousands of people praying for her, Erika stopped bleeding and came home for good. She will always be susceptible to the disease as she grows up, but she is very smart and very beautiful as are all our girls.

45

9/11/2001

Erika's second birthday, 9/11/2001, will live in infamy. I sat on a plane due to leave KC for Dallas. None of us were aware of why the plane sat at the gate for so long. Then, after waiting for 30 minutes or more we were asked to depart the plane with no reason given. But, some of the people on cell phones started to talk about a plane crash at the World Trade Center. The world stopped that day to watch and listen. Work was no longer of importance as they watched the second plane hit the South Tower. I was walking back into the office as this happened and people stared at the lobby TV screens in disbelief.

My peer on the East Coast was on a family vacation at this time. I volunteered to take the first week in Manhattan. We had a switch site about eight blocks from Ground Zero and all power to lower Manhattan was off. Three of the four generators on the site failed and Sprint sent three generators on trailers and sat them in the alley. These generators needed security, and it was my job to get them secured and assist getting employees and contractors through the checkpoints manned by military personnel. I flew into La Guardia on the following Thursday when the airlines were allowed to fly. As expected, the plane was nearly empty and La Guardia had little activity from travelers. I was working with Corporate Security to help co-ordinate the guard force.

The gentleman from Corporate was a retired NYPD Lieutenant

and had the connections needed with the chaos going on in lower Manhattan. I was not able to find a hotel in lower Manhattan because of the loss of power so I stayed in Midtown and took the Subway as close to the site as possible, then walked another three blocks to our PCS switch site where we maintained a shuttle van. All the guards had to work 12-hour shifts, and the change was done at 6:00am each day and again at 6:00pm. The guards coming on had to meet at the shuttle area at 5:00am and go through two check points before reaching the secured switch site. Then the out going guards had to ride the shuttle back then get transportation home from there.

After getting the guard force changed, I was responsible to pick up a Sprint PCS employee at Grand Central Station and get him through the check points and within two blocks of Ground Zero. I then walked him to the Sprint PCS bus which remained at Ground Zero as an area the workers could get into an air conditioned environment for a break, with food and drinks available, and free calls home to let their loved ones know they were okay. As I stood at Ground Zero looking at the devastation, it was hard to imagine it was the same area where Hope and I had taken family and friends to. We would go up to the World Trade Center observation deck to view the city and harbor. As I stood there, I looked at the unbelievable site; smelling and seeing the smoke still rising from a pile of rubble six stories high, steel beams hanging out of high rise buildings as if they were arrows shot by the devils bow, smaller buildings cut in half by chunks of steel from one of the WTC buildings.

My first morning after getting about three hours of sleep, found me standing on the train platform near midtown at 3:00am. There was no one else on the platform but I had company, a NY Rat going from trashcan to trashcan. As the train pulled into the station, it was empty. I got on and sat alone for two stops before reaching the end of the line, a point where the trains could go no further before reaching Ground Zero. I repeated this process for another night until I heard of a hotel that had opened only a few blocks from our switch site. I was able to move in and eliminate much of the travel hassle. Plus, I could check on the guards more often. We were able to get access to the headquarters set up in a local high school near Ground Zero. Volunteers from all across the country from police and fire stations were there awaiting instructions on what was needed. K-9 units to help in looking for survivors were no longer of use.

One night, after checking on the guards, I walked to Ground Zero. It was pitch black except for the lights run by generators at Ground Zero where personnel had begun the operation of removing the debris one truck at a time. It was very surreal, as I got closer, to see the six-story mountain at night and the shadows created by the search lights. This sight has been added to my memory banks as one that will always come up when the WTC is mentioned. I worked until the following Tuesday and was relieved to go home. Home with Hope and the girls and sleep in my own bed.

46

Last Year with Sprint

The following year I knew would be my last with Sprint. My position was being moved to Las Vegas and the pay grade dropped two levels. Also, there would be no relocation package. This situation made the decision to leave even easier. Hope and I had already discussed that we could not move Sarah and Jackie to the West Coast where they would finish high school and go to college. Chances are they would end up living and working there and our family would be split in half; rarely getting the ability to all be together for a reunion. I knew refusing the move would mean being laid off, but I was ready to move the family back to Georgia with a chance Sprint would need a security person in Atlanta. That would never happen.

As I traveled my last year with Sprint I made sure to finish my work and see things in the West I had wanted to visit. One day while leaving the San Francisco sales office I decided to drive by the new baseball stadium. As I approached, I saw there was going to be an afternoon game with a 4:00 start. The team playing the Giants that day was the Atlanta Braves. I took that as a sign, parked the rental car and headed for the ticket window. I never sat in the seat; I just roamed the new stadium, walked the right field wall and looked out over McCovey Bay. Later I sat near the bullpen and watched Greg Maddux warm up for the Braves. The Braves won the game and it made for a great trip.

One of my favorite places to visit was the Portland, Oregon area and up the Columbia River to Hood River. Hood River is a great small town sitting on the river with Mt. Hood in its back yard. A must stop along I-84 interstate is Multnomah Falls, a 620 foot falls with a walking bridge at the base of the main falls. There is no hiking needed. Once you pull into the parking lot you are there.

Another stop just north of Portland into Washington is Mt. St. Helens. I had never visited this area but after leaving Hood River and heading North to see some of the smaller towns we serviced, I checked the map and found an observation area I could drive to on the West side of the mountain. Driving alone into this area was very eerie and as the road neared the eruption site, the trees disappeared. Or, I should say they were all laying flat as if they were chopped down all in the same direction. By this time, there were bushes and smaller trees growing but the devastation was obvious. As I drove around the slopes of the mountain, I could see areas of the road that had caved in and had to be re-built. Once at the viewing area I realized I wasn't dressed for the cold windy conditions but that didn't matter. I stared directly into the crater just a short distance away.

I looked down onto Spirit Lake that was still there but full of floating logs. I remember the story about Harry Truman, the mountain man who ran a small fishing lodge on the lake. Truman and his lodge would have disintegrated from the initial blast and be buried under the huge wall of mountain ash. On the opposite side of the crater is the Johnston Ridge Observatory where David A. Johnston stood as the eruption began. He would have just seconds to live. Mt. St. Helens should not be missed if you travel to the Portland area.

My next trip to California and the San Jose area I decided to visit Monterey Bay and Pebble Beach. It was late afternoon as I arrived at the famous golf course and had a surprise. Workers were in the process of moving a giant Cypress tree to replace the 18th green tree, which had died. They were moving the tree across the 16th fairway as I arrived. The huge tree with at least a 15-foot deep root ball was mounted on a self-leveling trailer and held in place with cables. The trailer was pulled with a Caterpillar while workers placed 4x8 pieces of plywood in front of the Cat as they slowly moved along.

The course had been closed in the afternoon and the last foursome was teeing off on 17. I was given permission to tag along and followed the golfers on 17 and 18. It was a great feeling just to stand and lean against the wood rail on the 18th tee box and soak in the view. I followed the golfers until they finished 18 and went back to pick up the tree moving as it came down 17 and turned on the 18th fairway. It was getting dark by the time they were about half way to the 18th green. They shut down until the next day so I missed the final process of backing the tree into its final position and removing it from the trailer.

On my last trip to Southern California, I took Hope along for her to enjoy the weather and scenery. When I would stop at a Sprint PCS store for an assessment of its security, Hope would always have shops in the area to visit while I worked. While staying in San Diego, we had the opportunity to have a visit with one of my high school buddies, Bob Gannon, who had just returned from one of his flying adventures around the world. The next evening we had dinner with another high school buddy, Tom Beard and his wife Carol. Tom and Bob were in business together owning Shuttermart, a house shutter manufacturing company.

47

Back to Georgia

The first few days of January 2003 were my last few days of work for Sprint. Hope and I paid a mover for the transport of our belongings and ended up storing most of them in her sisters' basement in Georgia. Hope, I, and the girls moved into Chris and Mandy's basement to have time and find the right place to live. Hope home-schooled Sarah and Jackie so they would not have to change schools again once we determined where we would live. Our home in Overland Park sold within a few weeks so we were fortunate not to have to wait very long to have our equity from its closing.

What Hope and I didn't expect was the length of time it would take to find a new home. With Chris and Mandy in Acworth, we started looking north and west of Atlanta to find our home. We decided to stay in the country and not live in a sub-division with all the rules and regulations. What we were to find out was the difficulty in finding a home with the right property. Also, Hope was busy planning a 50th Anniversary party for her parents on July 26th and a wedding; Buffy was going to be Mrs. Gary Warren and the date of the wedding was set for August 9th.

Buffy and Gary had first met in middle school and were an item by their freshman year at Sprayberry High School. Hope remembered seeing Gary at the Homecoming football game and Buffy was on the

Homingcoming Court as a freshman. Gary was bragging about his girl-friend to the other guys, but he warned them about looking too close. They continued to date all through high school, but broke up once or twice while Buffy was at Georgia State getting a business degree.

While we lived in Florida, Buffy had come to visit with a new boy friend but Sarah and Jackie would have nothing to do with him. Throughout the stay Buffy was asked by both girls, "Where's Gary? Why isn't Gary here?" Sarah and Jackie had known Gary as Buff's boy-friend since they were old enough to understand the relationship. They were dead set against any new guy coming in to take his place. I am sure the poor kid was glad when he left and the relationship broke up a short time later.

As Hope and I looked for a home, Gary and Buffy were trying to find their first home as the wedding came nearer. One day Gary called and asked us to go with them to see a piece of property in Bartow County. The property was on Alford Road and was almost to the Floyd county line. It was four and a half acres and was all pasture land except for a lone pine tree and a small patch of trees. Gary and Buffy felt it was too far for them to commute to their jobs in Atlanta. As Hope and I continued to look for a home, we kept the land on Alford Road in the back of our minds.

As we continued the search it was becoming apparent we would have to decide on the property we wanted and start from scratch on a home. We had looked at nine and a half acres in Cave Springs, which was in Floyd County and about 20 minutes south of Rome. It was a beautiful piece of land with mature trees and shrubs around a brick home but the home was not what we wanted and its construction de-sign was not a good fit for renovation. By May we had given up and visited the Alford Road site again to see how a home would be situated. We walked the property and decided we would purchase the four and a half acres and contact the neighboring farmer for an additional acre of flat land on top of the hill. We closed on the four and a half acres by the end of May but waited to start building until we had spoken with the farmer. Initially he said he had four and a half acres next to ours and wanted to sell it as a whole and said he had someone interested. Time continued to drag as he stalled for the entire four and a half acres. We only wanted one acre, but he finally said he would sell us two acres; we accepted and closed on the property by mid July.

At that point in our marriage I had moved Hope fifteen times in our almost 28 years of marriage. From all the homes we had lived in she knew exactly what she wanted and she started to design the home on a 3D architecture software program. Once the plan was completed, we located an engineer/architect to verify the design. To our surprise, he said the design was structurally sound, and we contracted him to make the complete construction plans for a builder. Other than a few small changes the house was exactly what Hope wanted.

I started checking builders in the area and provided the plans to get five bids. When I received the bids, I was surprised to see a $100,000 difference from the highest to the lowest bid. In follow up with the highest bid @ $380,000 the man looked me in the eye and said he was worth it. Hope and I gathered individual bids from framers, roofers, bricklayers, plumbing, etc. and determined we could build the house if we were the general contractor for around $240,000. That was what we decided to do, and by the first of August we had the basement dug and the walls poured. There were many boulders that came out of the basement area, and I had them piled along the tree line trying to decide what I would do with them.

But, before any further construction took place, we attended the wedding of our daughter, Mary Elizabeth (Buffy) Thomas and Gary Wayne Warren on August 9, 2003. Hope and Mandy made the cake for the wedding which took place at the Catholic Church, Transfiguration, near Marietta. The reception was in the church hall so no one had to run around trying to find it. Jack Lacy and his girlfriend, Katie, attended along with Dan McCabe and his wife Brenda. We all had a great time at the reception with a full meal served to guests.

48

Building our Dream Home

Gary and his father Mike had a 30-foot hunting trailer used during deer season that sat on property between Macon and Savannah. Before the wedding, the three of us had made the trip down to pick it up and set it on the construction site on Alford Road. This would serve as home for Hope and I from August through October. The girls stayed with Mandy and Chris during construction.

Gary was a bidding supervisor for a Residential Builder and served as my construction manager helping me set up scheduling dates to keep the construction moving in the order beneficial to completion of the home. Many of the contractors came from those used by Gary so I had some type of leverage over them to do the job right and on time.

Hope and I had some of the best times while living in that little trailer. We were comfortable, we had a porta potty, and I had finished a 700-foot water line. Our routine at the end of each day was to drive a half hour to Mandy and Chris' to see everyone, take a shower, change clothes, and eat. Then we drove back to the trailer to stay overnight and be a deterrent from anyone trying to come on the property and steal anything.

The roof for the house and garage was all trusses so once the framing started things moved fast. We stubbed water lines and drains into the basement floor with the idea we could create living space in the walkout basement. The design was for two bedrooms, a kitchen, laundry room, full bath and an area for a family theater. The living space would be almost 2,000 sq. ft. in the basement with 600 sq. ft. of storage and mechanical room space.

The single story brick ranch had 2600 sq. ft. of living space with three bedrooms; an office that could be made into a 4th bedroom, the living room and kitchen was one large room, and a separate dining room to the left of the foyer. The master bedroom was on one end and the other two bedrooms at the other end with two full baths at that end. A half bath was off the hall leading to the master suite, there was a large laundry room with cabinets and a full sink, and a door to the garage all from the back hall. A large pantry came off the kitchen with cabinets, storage shelves, and an area for the coffee maker, toaster, and a second microwave. The kitchen was framed with corian countertops and an island in the center was covered with a granite top.

At the end of the family room stood a huge fireplace using the same bricks as the outside of the house. The fireplace had a sitting bench the full length and then wrapped under a window next to the fireplace. The brick went to the top of the 14-foot ceiling with a built in archway to store firewood. It ran over budget from our original plan but the outcome was well worth the extra money.

Off the kitchen was a breakfast area with French doors that opened to a concrete porch covered with a roof and overlooking the back yard. The trussed roof covered the front porch with six large white pillars placed for looks only. The house sat at an angle from the road about 600 feet off the paved road. One wing was created with a three-car garage with a walk up stairs to an attic over the garage. This created plenty of storage that we used to its fullest.

One thing Hope did not want was carpeting. We decided on Brazilian Cherry hardwood flooring over the entire house except tile was placed in the bathrooms and laundry. Hope and I decided to install the hardwood flooring our selves. It was hard work, but we were able to take our time and select the pieces of wood where we wanted them to go. Brazilian Cherry comes in all colors and grains from almost blond to black. Each bundle was carried into the house and set in the rooms to sit for about two weeks to allow the wood to adapt to the temperature and humidity. As each bundle was opened it was like opening a present to see the grains and color combinations. Hope would cut any pieces as needed and move the pieces as I started on one side of the house and worked across the room into the kitchen and through the arched doorways. I had a couple of sleepless nights wondering how I would go through two different doorways and meet up into the foyer and dining room. The worry was for not as the lines came together perfectly and continued to the far wall. Once finished, the man who came to sand and finish the floor said it was laid better than any he had ever seen.

The tile was another matter and required knee work. I switched with Hope so she laid and grouted the tile while I carried and cut. What a team! Except when it came to playing cards, Hope is a social card player and I am out to kill. When playing four-point pitch I did okay, but Gin Rummy was another matter. If we played ten games, Hope would win eight or nine out of the ten games. We kept playing until I was so pissed I had to go to work. Sorry, but that is the way I am. Some coach, Herman Edwards I believe, said, "You play to win the game!" He was talking about football but I apply it to any game. I don't care if it is crazy eights, spoons, or the longest pissing contest. I just thought I could beat Hope in a pissing contest for sure.

Other features special in the house were things such as foam insulation on all outside walls to stop all air leaks. We put in a hot water pump that circulated hot water throughout the lines in the house. The electric bill might have been a little higher, but we did not waste water waiting for it to heat up to shave or shower. Our heating system was a dual heater that ran off a heat pump until it got below 40 degrees F, and then a conventional burner kicked in using propane. We had a 500-gallon propane tank buried in the ground for aesthetics rather than have the tank sitting alongside the house. We also had two 50-gallon water heaters; this was for the purpose of three females with long hair all getting ready in the morning at the same time.

I kept thinking about putting a fish/Koi pond in the back yard adjacent to the porch. I had built my first pond in Overland Park and we had enjoyed it tremendously. In Overland Park I had rented a small backhoe that sat on tracks to dig the pond. The problem there was more rocks than dirt to dig and I was sitting on a slope. The Backhoe did not have outriggers to help keep it stable, so I had to be careful. Prior to digging the pond I had paid a contractor to move huge flat lime stones into my yard to help with the drainage and to give some planting areas. As he dug into the hillside for the basement next door, huge flat rocks would be broken off. I paid $125 for five such rocks that averaged around six to eight feet in diameter and were probably two feet thick. Two such rocks were at the bottom of my fishpond. As I dug the hole, the bucket got hung up, and the backhoe tilted sharply up on one track. I was at a point where if I made the wrong move the backhoe was going over on its side onto the aforementioned rocks. I unbuckled my seatbelt and made a move with the levers; it was the wrong move. I was able to climb out the opposite door as the backhoe fell onto the rocks with a boom. It shook the ground enough Hope felt it in the house. She sent one of the girls to see if I was okay and I was, but I was done digging for a while.

When I called the rental company, they evidently were not surprised and sent out a large forklift to put the backhoe up right. They took that one back and brought me another one, smaller and with outriggers. All this for no extra charge, I guess they were glad I had not killed myself and felt themselves lucky.

Once the main part of the pond was dug, I attempted to drive the unit across to the next lot where I could go up and out of the drop off onto the street. Problem was, it had rained, and the backyard was mud with no grass. As I went one foot sideways, I would slide three feet farther down the slope and finally had to stop to keep from falling into a twenty foot crevice where a storm drain emptied. Another phone call to the rental company and out a man came with a trailer. He maneuvered the backhoe around the hole using the bucket and onto the trailer he went, no extra charge. They were just damn glad I was done.

Back to the pond, I wanted as natural of a pond as I could get, so I had created an upper hole to filter the water rather than use a mechanical filter. The hole was about three feet deep and five feet in diameter. The entire hole was lined with a rubber bladder type material. I had the pump line go into a drainage pipe that circled the bottom. A drainage pipe has holes along it to allow water to be dispersed evenly. I buried this pipe with pea gravel sized rock almost to the top of the hole.

I lined the lower pond and along a ten-foot stream, which dropped about five feet from the top hole to the main pond which was about three feet deep at the stream end that gradually came to about ten inches deep at the end. I had found a perfect flat rock to create a waterfall from the stream into the pond. With a lot of trial and error, I had a nice Koi pond with a stream and waterfall. Now it was time to buy the fish. Hope and the girls were involved in picking out some small Koi and different types of gold fish to go into the pond. I believe we ended up with three small Koi and another dozen gold fish.

I had to let the water circulate for about three days prior to putting the fish in the water. This was to allow the chlorine to evaporate out of the water; chlorine is deadly to the fish. I was able to add a little water with the hose every two or three days without hurting the fish.

One day I took a Friday off because the kids were off school and so was Hope. She had started working at the elementary school where Sarah and Jackie went to make extra money and she would have time off when they did. We had decided to go to a movie then grab something to eat before going home. When I stepped out back to look at the pond Hope was already there looking at all our fish belly up. She turned and looked at me with that "dumb ass" look in her eyes. I had started to top the water off in the pond before going to the movies and forgot to shut the hose off. As I said before, too much chlorine is not good for fish. So another trip was made to re-stock the pond.

Having learned the basics with the pond in KC I put together a plan for another pond at our new home. We all enjoyed sitting by the pond and watching the fish, frogs, and an occasional turtle.

At the new home, I had a nice flat area that drained away from the house. I didn't have a slope like in Kansas to build an upper area and stream down to the lower level so I decide to create one. After back filling around the basement, there was a good amount of dirt left over. I used a skid loader to pile the remaining dirt into a large cone. Rocks that came out of the basement were piled not far away, so I sorted the rocks by size using the skid loader. One rock was twice the size of any other rock and I decided to place it at the top of the pile of dirt.

I now had a plan in mind using the large rock as the main feature of the pond. I would swell the dirt away from the rock creating a moat type structure around it. I then created a dam of dirt at one point in the moat. I knew I had to force the water to move around the rock and then force it down a short stream of 10-15 feet to a second pond below. I used the large rock as support to build a small waterfall of about 20 inches.

I moved the next larger size of rocks to outline the pond and provide the support the rubber liner would need once filled with water, creating the lower pond. I had plenty of extra dirt available to haul up from the lower portion of the property where a drainage ditch had been dug. With the dirt filling in around the rocks and a natural slope down the hill away from the house provided a perfect place to create the over flow.

The pond needs an over flow to handle the extra water from rain storms. The great thing about rain; it provides a natural cleansing of the water. The other great thing was our county water was not treated with chlorine—I couldn't make a mistake like in Kansas. Hope and the fish were happy about that.

Once I got the rocks in place and dirt filed in I was ready to buy the rubber liner. The rubber liner comes 15 feet wide and in a roll so you simply roll out how long of a piece you need at the store, such as Home Depot. I needed three separate rolls about 30 feet in length. I was able to over lap each roll so I had only one small seam to seal that would be under water. Once done, I was able to cut the liner to fit over the top rock and had pieces left over to create a stream from the top moat to the lower pond. Once completed, I was ready to install a pump in the deep end of the lower pond next to the overflow. Using poly pipe that is somewhat flexible, I was able to connect the pump to the upper waterfall. I made a few changes after about three years, but the pond performed great and provided years of entertainment.

The final touches meant hiding the lining to make the pond look like it had been there for a long time. Plants were added in and around the pond to create an even more natural look. Now it was time for the fish. We weren't able to move any of our fish from Kansas so we gave most of them to friends that had a pond but no fish. Hope and I scoured the pet stores around Rome and Cartersville and came up with about 20 fish that included four Koi and the rest were shubunkin, fantail, comets, and regular gold fish. We put all 20 in the lower pond but later I decided to put five fish on top. The next day when I came outside, four of the fish were back in the bottom pond. One small fantail evidently said, "You guys are crazy to shoot the rapids!" Each time I moved fish to the top they would make their way down the stream to the lower pond but without us ever seeing it happen.

As with any pet you have to come up with names. These are the names I can recall. The largest black and white Koi was called "Dalmatian," a smaller black and white was "Puppy." A gold and black Koi I named "Goldie Hawn;" it turned out later that Goldie was a boy. A solid white Koi with a small orange dot on the head was called "Spot." And, a black, white, and red Koi was called "Lucy" because it had a red head; Lucy also turned out to be a boy. The comets are a type of gold fish with white markings and white tails. One was completely white on the belly with a red/orange top so we called it "Shamu." Others were called "Ghost," "Angel," "Horse," "Swirly Girl." I stopped moving the fish to the top so one fantail was there by herself, but not for long. When spring came the females started to get large bellies from eggs and the males would chase the females relentlessly pumping them nonstop. This is how we were able to determine males from females; Spot and Dalmatian were both female. As eggs were laid it is my understanding that the fish eat most of them. Some eggs get pushed under rocks and crevices so we were able to see baby fish arrive the first spring. And, because there was only one fish on top the eggs that were pumped to the top were safe. We ended up with almost 20 babies in the moat. The majority of the fish born on top were Koi. The funny thing is the fish born on top never attempted to go down stream to the lower pond. I guess they considered it home and had no desire to leave. You could see from the colors that they were offspring of Spot and Dalmatian.

Now back to the home construction. Hope and I moved into the basement by October because we had electricity and could use a space heater as nights got colder. Gary needed the trailer for deer season so the timing worked out good. Hope and I had created a nice bedroom area in one corner of the basement. We put up tarps for privacy, and to not make it too obvious that we were living there. By code it was illegal for us to stay there but we were builder/owners so it was not an issue for our county inspector. We were still using the porta potty so those early morning visits by November and December made for a quick in and out.

Once all the electrical and plumbing fixtures were in place we were able to get our occupancy permit and planned to move in once the wall painting was complete. Problems with our cabinetmaker had delayed us by almost three months but the quality made up for our frustration. He was extremely busy keeping full time builders happy so our time line kept being pushed back. After much persuasion and self imposed fines for any further delays, he came through and finished. We moved our belongings in February of 2004 and Sarah and Jackie had a home.

I had a great time planning the lay out for our landscaping. Red Azaleas were the main bushes planted on both sides of the front porch and side entry. At both ends of the porch, we planted River Birch trees, and at each side of the walk out basement, we planted Mimosa trees brought from mom and dad's property in Roberta, Georgia. One day while looking at plants at Wal-mart I went through some new roses just delivered. Each rose bush was named and when I found one called "Hopie Girl," I knew that was a sign. The blooms were yellow, and I had a perfect site along the south wall of the house next to the pond. About two years later Hope was able to find another Hopie Girl rose bush.

During a day trip with Bill and Anna, we found a great place north of Rome called the "Lily Patch." We were able to get a variety of day lilies and some oriental lilies as well. I completed the lily areas by adding some from a plant catalog.

One of the things we planned for during construction was that mom and dad would sell their property in Roberta, and then move onto our property once a doublewide trailer was in place. Mom's sister had passed away from cancer and mom wanted to be closer to family. We were able to get the zoning board to allow a guest home as long as the main home provided the water and electric feeds. Hope was gracious in her decision to share our property with my parents. Mom and dad were both having health problems, and we knew it would be better having them close rather than a two hour drive away.

Once they purchased the doublewide, and it was set on the property, they wanted to add a deck onto the back. Gary and his father Mike Warren helped get the main deck and roof up then Dad and I were able to finish shingling the roof and finish the rails and steps. Dad purchased a carport, and I finished their drive with gravel using the skid loader. The neighbor let us use their tractor and plow and a garden was created just beyond the carport and driveway.

Hope and I spent much of our time helping mom and dad get setup with new doctors in Rome. Dad had cancer in his bladder while in Roberta so it was something the doctors needed to keep an eye on. Dad had a tough year starting in 2005 because they decide to remove his bladder and prostrate but needed to fix an aneurysm in one of his arteries near his lower back area first. They had to go through his abdominal area to get to it, which made for a tough recovery. As soon as he had recovered enough then they planned his bladder and prostrate surgery so he was right back in the hospital again. His surgery went well but after coming home it was determined he had developed a serious staff infection. So, he was back in the hospital for another two weeks for treatment. When he was sent home, he was sick within a week and it was the same staff infection. So, he went back into the hospital for another two weeks. It was the worst for him but mom, Hope, and I were also tired of running back and forth to the hospital everyday over a three-month period.

It took dad nearly a year and a half before he started to get his strength back. He was able to get a machine to help him sleep at night after he was diagnosed with sleep apnea. When he would wear it he slept better and seemed to gain strength. The biggest problem was the increase of pills needed by both mom and dad. With the cost of medicine alone, they were spending well over half of their Social Security money. Hope was able to research and after many days of calling and filling out paper work she was able to eliminate their medicine payments. Pharmaceutical companies had programs for low income people to get free pills; they just didn't advertise that fact. But, as soon as Medicare came out with the new drug programs, the free plans from the Pharmaceuticals were cancelled. This put the folks right back into a financial bind because of co-pays and yearly limits.

49

Dark Days Ahead

Since moving into the home, I had started applying for jobs feeling with my degree and background I would be able to find something in the Atlanta North Metro area. It would make for a tough commute, but living in the country would make it worth the hassle. I did not realize the job market had already begun to tighten; especially for a man almost 54. Within the next year I had only two interviews for a Security Manager and a Security Director position. The director position was down to three people for the interview process with a salary of 100-110K per year. It would have made our plan to move back to Georgia a financial success, but I was not selected. After that, job opportunities for that level of security became almost obsolete.

Companies began moving to the Internet for the application process, which made it difficult to get a foot or toe in the door. Without that face-to-face impression it makes it easy for a company to eliminate just based on resume information. Maybe the EEOC is working on a formula to prove age discrimination exists. I believe it does, just based on the fact older workers create high medical costs and higher life insurance premiums. Now I am sixty five years old with the prospects of getting a high paying job even slimmer as each year goes by.

The jobs that are available are the commission only ones. Believe me, I tried many of them over the past several years; selling leased security equipment, high price lighting equipment, GPS equipment, telecommunication services, etc. When I decided to go with life insurance, I was told it was a two-year commitment. I gave it three and failed to make enough to pay utilities much less all the bills.

But, hind sight is 20/20, and I made too many mistakes from the start. The decision to leave Sprint was the right choice because it allowed Hope and I to raise Sarah and Jackie close to their older sisters. But, I reacted too much to loosing 75% of my 401K in about a year's period. When the Dot.com's went down the telecom stocks went with them. But, each management meeting declared the stock would rebound and confirmation was repeated by those trust worthy brokerage firms. By the time the stock dropped from $100 to $25 per share I had enough and moved everything to low risk funds. That was a good move because the stock didn't stop until under $3 a share.

What I did was take a lump sum on the 401K and my pension and use the money to build our home thinking I could recover with a good job. But, tax time came in 2004 and I was responsible for $150K in state and federal taxes. This was paid by taking a mortgage on the property for more money than I ever had on any of our other homes. The $75,000 we had in equity from the Overland Park home allowed us to keep going while the job search continued. Hope took a job again as a paraprofessional for Special Education students that mainly provided us with health insurance. My retirement health benefits did not even cover one year. When I called the benefits line, I was told I could not use the money for a partial year and had to pay the difference to get a year of coverage. I asked to speak to the director, and she told me I had two choices. Pay the difference or get some other plan on my own. I guess she was pissed because all of her stock options were worthless. That was another loss I hadn't mentioned yet. Once upon a time, as a manager level, I was given options as a choice on our yearly bonus. I always took the options rather than the cash. My options at one point were valued at over $100K but I was only able to squeeze out about 15-20K out of them before they all became worthless.

So, my problems financially were of my own doing. I had no one but myself to blame. And, as time went by, I started to have nightmares of retreating into a corner with no way out. Just as I would gain some confidence that things would turn around, they turned for the worse.

I had started to make money in the insurance side by selling mortgage protection insurance. There were plenty of good leads purchased through an agency. But, as the economy started to fall the mortgages came to a fast halt. And the policies I had already sold began to be cancelled as jobs were lost. There is a thing in the insurance business called "charge backs." This meant any commissions already paid on dropped policies would be taken back from future sales commission. Plus, a percentage of the commission you were to receive a year down the road would never materialize.

At that time, I was desperately looking for another job, any kind of job to help pay the bills. A County Sheriffs' department was looking for jailers that would pay less than $25k per year but that was better than nothing. I went through the interview process and even though I was over qualified for the position I thought it would allow me to move up into management as positions became available. Plus, the benefits were good. Part of the hiring process at the end was a polygraph exam. As each person went into the exam, we were told we would be hired as soon as the exam was finished and H.R. was aware of the results. We would receive a call from H.R. on when we would start. As I took the exam, I was fine until I was asked if I had ever stolen anything. My mind was blank as I tried to remember anything. I should have said yes, but I didn't recall any particular event. I said no to the question and I could tell the examiner did not like my response. I was told the results of the exam and mentioned the question to Hope when I got home. "Well you told me you stole packs of cigarettes from your dad." I never got a call back from the sheriff's department and they would not respond to my messages. I guess cigarettes are not only hazardous to your health, but also bad for getting hired. It probably came back to how my sub-conscious was harmed when I participated as a look out for Uncle Tom during the great cigarette theft at the family re-unions.

I joke now, but it wasn't a joke at the time. Of one job I knew I should have gotten that job was it. I guess all things are supposed to happen for the better according to the Master Gurus of the world. I am still trying to figure that one out.

A buddy of mine, who I met after the service, was living in Florida. He was in Vietnam with the same Marines unit, at the same time I was there but in Fox Company and not Hotel Company. I had received an email form him many times over the years to come to the 2/1 reunions. I had not been able to afford it but he mentioned wanting to talk to me about a job opportunity. The reunion was in Houston, Texas and the city was going to recognize the 2nd Battalion 1st Marine Division and we would march in the Veterans Day parade.

I went just to here about the job opportunity but as soon as I checked into the hotel, I had bad news from home. Jackie had collapsed at basketball practice, and she was taken to the hospital with a seizure that would not stop. She was finally given medication after two and a half hours that brought it under control. Multiple tests later were not able to find a cause. Hope said I should, so I stayed in Houston and enjoyed the reunion. The parade was a great thing for all of us Vietnam Veterans. We were toward the end of the parade and the crowds roared as they became aware of us. It was worth the trip to Houston.

Later in the year, I went to Florida to visit with my Marine friend and stayed in his home for a couple of days. He was doing well in his business providing services to car dealerships. One of the things he was interested in and had signed a marketing agreement for was a GPS unit that would provide similar services as Onstar for GM vehicles. The product was geared for dealers who wanted to offer such services. I was to try to open the Georgia market and work strictly on commissions. Again, I could see a way out of my financial situation if I could get the product in some dealerships. Once it caught on I could go anywhere I wanted for more dealers.

Once I started speaking with dealers I found interest in the product but more concern about car sales. As the weeks progressed, I had not one dealer signed up. By that time, dealers were laying people off or totally going out of business. I was on another roller coaster ride; hopes up, hopes down. And, this time I kept descending as I got no answer and no response on any job applications. And, when the housing market collapsed I found we were upside down with our home.

Before this, I was able to fight back and keep my emotions under control. But, as each day went by and bills were paid with the last savings we had left, my thoughts turned dark. There was no need to blame anyone but myself. I had created this problem with the thought I could turn it around. I was wrong.

As my thoughts became darker I kept coming back to the fact I was worth more dead than alive. I had taken out a $300K life insurance policy for 15 years with a return of premium rider. That means I would get a return of everything I paid into the policy once the 15-year period ended. If I dropped the policy, everything I paid would be lost, and we could no longer afford the monthly premiums.

I started thinking about suicide. I kept thinking that Hope would recover from my death and have the money to stay in the home. Plus, my parents were going to lose their home as well. But, my only concern was for Hope and the girls. I knew Hope could find a loving husband.

As I drove anywhere, I would find myself thinking about a car accident. I started looking on the Internet and reading stories about people who had committed suicide. In each case I would think about how I might commit suicide with the least amount of shock to my family. Who would find me? Where should I go? I was a failure. I had lost everything that Hope and I had worked for all these years of marriage. My parents would lose their home and where would they go? Why did this happen? Why couldn't I prevent it?

The last monthly premium had been paid. Now I had to make a decision. The policy would no longer be any good in 30 days. I was beginning to understand how someone must feel before committing suicide. How lonely or scared they must be. Their health has failed them physically and then it begins to affect their mental health. I knew I was wrong to think the way I was. I kept getting pushed farther into the corner with no way out and my thoughts kept coming back to one solution. I stood in the bathroom with my hand full of pain pills. Would this be enough to kill me? Everyone was gone to work or school. I stared as in a trance into my hand. Then, I was startled by a loud noise in the house. Someone must be home. I put the pills back and went through the house. No one was there. What had I heard? I had been too close and now I understood I had to get help. I knew this was not the right answer. I could not think of hurting Hope and the girls this way.

I made an appointment with my VA Doctor by telephone. She set up an appointment for me to see a psychiatrist. After meeting with the doctor, she asked if she could speak to my wife. I agreed, feeling she could explain things better to Hope. I knew she would be hurt. As the doctor spoke with Hope by telephone later that day, I felt no emotion. The doctor had provided me with a heavy dose of antidepressant that dulled any shame I should have felt. What I didn't know until later was the doctor wanted to place me in a mental ward until she felt the medication was going to work. Hope convinced her to let me stay at home.

I had told the doctor I knew I was wrong and needed help. I had made the decision to do what was needed to stay with my family. We were losing material things, but we still had our health and most importantly, each other.

It was hard to tell mom and dad they would have to move. They were settled and any change like this would be extremely difficult. As it turned out, my cousin in Musella, Georgia had a tenant move out of the trailer his mother had lived in. This was mom's half sister and was back in the area they had moved from. They were able to get moved, and I set out to try to sell their trailer. Fortunately, I became aware of a man near Jasper, Georgia who was interested in buying the trailer to move onto property he owned for rental income. The price was well below normal value but it provided mom and dad the extra money they would need down the road.

Hope and the girls sat down with me and we discussed my mental problems. I told them I would be okay and promised I would no longer think as before. Family was more important to me, and Hope and I would somehow get by. Hope had once told me, years before; she would live with me in a tent. I was hoping it would not come to that. But, we had to find another place to live, and I needed to find a job because we couldn't even afford to pay utilities any longer.

Hope and I worked to have a yard sale to get some income and get rid of things we would no longer need. I was concerned about what to do with the fish and ran an ad on one of the Internet sales sites. Fortunately, I received a call from Mike who had lost all the fish in one of his ponds due to a lightning strike. Once Mike saw my set up, we agreed on a price for the fish and the entire pond, liner and all. Mike even purchased some of the small trees and bushes in the yard. Mike had land in the Jasper area and had been working on land development until the economy went bad. He had other ponds with Koi on his property so I felt comfortable with him getting the fish. Some of the new Koi went to a local friend who had built a pond the year before. His pond turned out great and the fish would have a nice home.

Mom and dad had a home, and the fish had a home. Now it was time for Hope, Me, Sarah, and Jackie to have a home. Sarah was already studying at Georgia Southern so the change would not affect her as much as Jackie. Jackie was going to start her senior year at Woodland High School and I knew it would not be a stable time for her. Hope and I kept looking at rental property in Bartow County, but things did not look good.

Mandy called one day and asked if I wanted to work at the Bentwater Golf Course. She was teaching Sunday school with the General Manager of the course and he had mentioned he was looking for someone. Once I met him, it was a done deal, and I had a job. I began working in the Pro Shop and helped with the cart staff when needed. It was enjoyable work, but the hours were affected by the weather. The hours varied from week to week but again it was money we were desperate for. More than anything, the job gave me a sense of purpose; I was actually doing something to help.

With our debts beyond anything we could hope to pay off we contacted an attorney to prepare for bankruptcy; something I never dreamed we would have to go through. With Hope's help, the law firm was able to complete the paperwork and set a court date. The process was fairly smooth, and I was not surprised with the volume of people in the same circumstance as we were. It was a true relief to have the bankruptcy finalized and put us in a position to plan our future.

With our financial situation, I continued to use the VA system. After a few months, the Psychiatrist put me in touch with a VA counselor in Atlanta. After meeting with the counselor and talking through my Vietnam experiences he asked if I had applied for PTSD benefits (Post Traumatic Stress Disorder). I had not so he advised me to start the paperwork to request for benefits. The process can take a year or more so it's important to get the process started.

Before going any further, I have to back up and look at what I thought to be a trap in a corner with no way out. What I came too close to doing not only to myself but also to the entire family. If there is a lesson to be learned it is that nothing is as bad as it appears to be at the time. Things will work themselves out in some way. I am not happy with what has happened but in the end, it has made me appreciate family and friends more. I would have missed the birth of two more grandsons, Cole Riley Warren and Ty Weston Warren. Watching all the grandchildren grow is a joy as they reach their goals and dreams. And, the one person I owe the most to is Hope.

Hope is small in stature and therefore has what is called the "short person syndrome." They have to talk loud to be noticed, and that is Hope. She is the person at the movie who thinks something is funny but is the only one laughing—LOUD. The rest of the audience laughs because of her laugh. And there is no mistake, if you know Hope; you would recognize it is her. But I tease only because I love her so much.

When I first met her, I knew she was special, and I fell in love with her within days. Hope taught me how to love someone and not be afraid to show your love. My family, like many of the families I knew growing up, did not show their love in public and would never say I love you. I had never been told I was loved in words, but I knew or felt my parents loved me. That is how they were raised and how they raised their three boys. I had never told my parents "I love you" until after being married to Hope for two or three years. But she showed me how it should be and I finally learned a valuable lesson. Don't be afraid to tell someone you love them, you may miss the chance. I loved my brother Larry but never spoke the words for him to hear.

Hope also showed me how to be positive in life and make your own happiness. I believe that was my gift to her, I made her happy. I have always made her laugh and try to tell her I love her each day. She is my happiness, and that is what came through in my darkest hour when I thought of taking my own life, thoughts of her saved my life. But I have always thought she saved my life. She turned my life into something beautiful and became my best friend. So after reflecting on our time together I can't imagine life being any better than my life with Hope. We will keep on keeping on as long as we both shall live. I will always love you Hope.

CPSIA information can be obtained
at www.ICGtesting.com
Printed in the USA
LVOW12s2039070416

482612LV00001B/122/P